THE
DESTROYERS

Rachel Notley and the NDP's war on Alberta

Rebel News Network Ltd.
Toronto, ON

Sheila Gunn Reid

Rebel News Network Ltd.

PO Box 73536, Wychwood PO
Toronto, ON M6C 4A7

Copyright © 2015 Rebel News Network Ltd.

ISBN 978-0-9950168-0-4

TABLE OF CONTENTS

ACKNOWLEDGEMENTS

I'd like to thank my loving family and generations of Albertans that came before me. They've demonstrated the value of the prairie work ethic; that hard work, self reliance and a strong sense of community leaves little room for government interference.

Thank you to Kevin Libin for his research and editorial assistance.

Photos are courtesy of Canadian Press, used with permission.

FOREWORD

Rachel Notley never thought she'd be the premier of Alberta. She seemed quite content being a perpetual dissident, the leader of the rump NDP opposition, a permanent protester who happened to have a seat in the provincial legislature and a government paycheque.

It was the family business. Her late father, Grant Notley, was also NDP leader, a rare socialist voice in Canada's most entrepreneurial province.

In hundreds of Question Period exchanges and street protests, Notley never indicated a desire to actually lead the province she so clearly delighted in hectoring. It wasn't just politically impossible. It made no sense. Wannabe Alberta premiers don't wear Che Guevara watches; they don't hire Greenpeace disruptors as their staff.

Alberta's parliamentary system, inherited from the United Kingdom, is built on the premise of a "loyal opposition" – politicians who zealously oppose and disagree with the government of the day, but have an underlying loyalty to Queen and country. But more than forty years of one-party rule in Alberta blurred the line between the Progressive Conservatives and the province itself. And so the NDP's rage blurred, too. Sometimes their anger was directed towards to the Progressive Conservatives, or the government. But sometimes it seemed like the NDP actually hated Alberta itself – or at least its leading industries and institutions. That anti-Alberta hostility was hard to miss when the NDP held international press conferences to denounce the oilsands – protests clearly designed to turn world opinion against Alberta, rather than to woo Alberta voters for the NDP. And Notley displayed no deep loyalty to the province, moving to B.C. for nearly a decade when NDP fortunes there were better.

In opposition, Notley and her small band of MLAs had the best of both worlds: the freedom to be radical activists, with no responsibility to actually govern.

And then the accidental election happened.

In a staggering political miscalculation, Alberta's two dominant conservative parties cooked up a secret, back-room deal to merge – short-circuiting the democratic process and abandoning conservative policies. Voters were disgusted – at the PC party for yet another back-room deal, and another un-conservative budget. And at the Wildrose leadership for agreeing to euthanize the province's opposition for political favours.

Jim Prentice, the PC premier, panicked, and called a snap election. Voters snapped back – voting for the only leader who didn't seem tainted by the fiasco. Albertans knew nothing about Notley, other than she carried herself well in the provincial leaders' debate. And that was good enough for them.

The NDP – which was signing up sacrificial candidates literally weeks before election day – stormed into office. In a major exit poll, 93% of Albertans said they were simply voting for change; only 7% said they wanted NDP policies. But that's not how it works in elections. You don't get to tack on conditions to your ballot.

What has come next has been shocking to those 93% of Albertans: the full brunt of the NDP. Not just Notley and her Alberta protesters. But every NDP mercenary from across Canada, streaming towards Alberta to help bring the province down a notch. It's an NDP dream: to de-Albertafy Alberta.

In The Destroyers, Sheila Gunn Reid looks at Notley, and the people behind Notley's throne – the radicals in caucus and cabinet. And just as important, the imported NDP activists, jetting in from Vancouver and Toronto for a tour of duty.

Any open-minded reader can come to only one conclusion: Rachel Notley hasn't changed. She's still the same radical activist she always was, who hates oil and gas, farming and ranching, and free enterprise.

She's not here to govern those things. She's here to destroy them.

Ezra Levant

INTRODUCTION

D on't listen to anyone who tries telling you that Albertans voted to elect an NDP government on May 5, 2015. They didn't. What voters really did was vote to un-elect a PC government.

We know that's true because **an Abacus poll** taken shortly after the vote found that an enormous 93 per cent of respondents said the result was "more about a desire for change rather than a preference for the NDP." Polls showed Rachel Notley's party trailing in the mid-teens just months before the election. Then came a few months of insulting, outrageous moves by the conservative leaders: The double-crossing by Wildrose leader Danielle Smith and her treacherous Wildrose MLA friends along with her accomplice, Progressive Conservative leader Jim Prentice; Prentice's terrible tax-and-spend budget, easily the worst up until then in Alberta's history; his snap-election scheme to kneecap a wounded Wildrose Party. Even NDP voters polled by Abacus were "as likely as everyone else to say it was more about change." Just seven per cent of Albertans believe we actually wanted an NDP government. Some mandate.

The NDP is an accidental government. Their electoral win was a cataclysmic mistake similar to a bad Vegas vacation. Canada's richest, most oil-dependent province lost control one night, and woke up the next morning to find itself married to a party of anti-capitalist, anti-oil radicals. Because make no mistake: that's what this party is. Whatever people think about the soft words and friendly face of Rachel Notley, there's extremism behind that smile.

Of course, the NDP radicals don't want to hear they were mistakenly elected in a fit of provincial pique. No one wants to believe that they were picked because they were the only daughter on the farm. They're already convincing themselves that Albertans are leading the country in a move to the far left. The Alberta results in the last federal election show that delusion couldn't be further from the truth. Albertans are still conservative.

While attending the Calgary Stampede, NDP leader **Thomas Mulcair said** of his chances in the federal election, "People have been looking at us very closely and the breakthrough here in Alberta followed a breakthrough in Quebec in the 2011 (federal) campaign. It really shows that the NDP does represent change." When Alberta's new Jobs Minister, Lori Sigurdson, left the province in the summer (during the worst jobs crisis in years, when unemployment rates in Fort McMurray doubled to over 8 per cent), she pitched in on the Okanagan-area campaign of far-left, federal NDP candidate Jacqui Gingras. Imagine the misplaced sense of confidence: A minister whose responsibility is the employment of Albertans throwing her time and support behind a politician who once called Alberta's largest employer, **the oil sands, "reckless."** Sigurdson told the local press that the so-called orange wave was coming from Alberta. "I think if you can win in Alberta, you can win anywhere," **she said.**

If only Mulcair was right — that people were looking at the NDP "very closely." The fact is, nobody in Alberta really looked at the NDP closely before the election. Not the media, who were too preoccupied with carefully combing through every ancient Tweet and Facebook post made by right-wing politicians. Not the voters, who had no idea they would wake up to a far-left, anti-oil government on May 6. Not even the NDP itself carefully vetted the NDP.

That's why they — and the rest of us — didn't start finding out about some of the nuts in their caucus until after the election. Worse yet, it wasn't the media that bothered to check out the fledgling caucus of NDP MLAs. It was citizens, fed up with the media, taking matters into their own hands. Then, and only then, did the media finally take notice. Just look at what happened with Deborah Drever. Less than three weeks after the election, Notley was removing her from the NDP caucus — not for something that Drever did after the election. But because Notley, along with the rest of Alberta, discovered all kinds of offensive and troubling stuff about Drever that was all over the Internet for anyone to see long before. The scandals started the **very day after the election** — as soon as anyone bothered to check: Drever celebrating marijuana use; Drever mocking rape victims in a photo shoot for a rock album; Drever making homophobic jokes; a post on her Facebook page of someone giving the finger to the Canadian flag.

That's pretty bad. But Drever's just a goofy kid. She's offensive and insensitive and foolish. But compared to many of the 53 other MLAs still in the NDP's caucus, and the damage they plan to do to Alberta, Drever's relatively harmless. Embarrassing? Oh yes, but fairly benign.

Compared to, say, Rod Loyola, elected as an Edmonton MLA in May and a communist defender of Venezuela's nutty strongman Hugo Chavez and a fan of Fidel Castro, who believes in "at least" tripling Alberta's oil royalties. He even once performed a rap song against capitalism. That's as embarrassing as Drever, but far less benign.

NDP MLA Colin Piquette has spoken at rallies that accuse Alberta's oil industry of perpetrating "genocide" against First Nations, posing with an upside-down, defaced Canadian flag. The message scrawled in marker across the Maple Leaf: "No blood for oil." Interesting stance, considering the alternative to Alberta's ethical brand of oil is bloody conflict oil. Piquette believes we're on "stolen land" and has said publicly that he's ashamed of his province. Yet here he is, part of the team running the show. He can't really be that ashamed.

Edmonton NDP MLA Deron Bilous is another

one eager to attack Alberta's energy employers. He has campaigned to pull from all Alberta classrooms energy literacy teaching materials provided by oil and gas companies, calling them **"outrageous and appalling."** He's also said the best way to grow the economy is to stop the oil sands, even advocating for no new approvals of oil sands projects. That's crazy. The economy doesn't work that way. But guess what? He's now the Minister of Economic Development and Trade.

Calgary NDP Jamie Kleinsteuber (who only lived in the city three months before being elected) is proud of being a genuine "socialist." Oh, good. I was worried he was one of those fake ones. That's actually pretty typical in this caucus. Edmonton NDP MLA David Shepherd, a cyclist and musician, has said Albertans "want" higher taxes; Calgary MLA Michael Connolly — who says the world "hates" Alberta because of the oil sands — supports a provincial sales tax, and a "super-tax" for the wealthy. They never do say who the wealthier are.

Still, those are just the kooky backbenchers. The terrifying reality is that the high-ranking NDPers, the ones that make all the real decisions in government, are just as radical. Actually, they're probably even more so.

There's Sigurdson, the jobs minister who, before she was elected, was speaking at events held by the anti-capitalist group Occupy Wall Street. She believes that low taxes are "ideological" and has visions for raising taxes by — are you sitting down? — $11 billion. She was an anti-poverty activist during her days as a social worker. It's a laudable cause. But I don't think she's cut from the "jobs are the best social program" cloth.

David Eggen, the minister of education and culture, is another fan of attending anti-oil sands rallies. And he's just one of the many NDPers who wants to bring oil sands development to a screeching halt. Except, naturally, he calls them tar sands — as most NDPers do. It's how you can tell what side they're on. "Doing the right thing means that we have no new approvals for tar sands projects," Eggen announced on his microphone at one rally, before leading the anti-oil crowd in a chant of "No New Approvals! No New Approvals!" Left-wingers sure love to chant.

Environment Minister Shannon Phillips will have a big role in regulating the oil sands and other energy developments. Before she was elected, she wrote a "radical" how-to book (even she calls it that), co-authored with Greenpeace's top Alberta campaigner and former Notley staffer Mike Hudema. The book celebrated lawbreaking environmental protests, like blockades and trespassing. Shannon Phillips compares Alberta to apartheid-era South Africa. I suppose that makes Notley the NDP version of Mandela. She's said she wants to hit the oil sector with higher royalties and use the money to "invest in a green economy" — as if Alberta could instead export billions of dollars worth of solar power.

Brian Mason, the minister of infrastructure and transportation, has labelled the impact of Alberta's oil sands (he calls them "tar sands," too) an "environmental embarrassment." Mason wants to stop developing the oil sands until someone comes along and builds the refineries to upgrade our crude. A new refinery hasn't been built in decades for a number of reasons, the most important being that it just doesn't make economic sense to the private sector to make the multi-billion dollar investment. And finding the willing and available private capital now could take years, of course; what he really wants is those awful "tar sands" just to stop. Waiting for that magical value added project to come along and suddenly make that dirty old oil clean is just an excuse to stop the industry.

When Finance Minister Joe Ceci was a Calgary alderman, he championed getting the city's investments out of oil companies, who don't satisfy his environmental righteousness. "We should be able to say to Calgarians that we're investing in things that are contributing to a positive world ... If environmental factors on some of the companies out there are less than sustainable, then we should not be investing in those areas." So, in the Alberta finance minister's opinion, our energy sector doesn't "contribute to a positive world." Ceci was also an anti-poverty activist and former social worker. If this sounds familiar, it should. Ceci even spoke at conferences with current jobs minister Sigurdson back in their social justice days. The irony is that antipoverty activists today would find themselves lots of work in Joe Ceci's Alberta. Unemployment and food bank usage is spiking while the energy industry sees round after round of layoffs.

And then there's our premier, Rachel Notley. She also wants to "slow down" the oil sands indefinitely. She, too, shows up at anti-oil rallies — this is the now-premier of Alberta! — where people march with signs reading "no tar sands, no tankers, no pipelines." She did more than just show up. She spoke, rather passionately, at these anti-Alberta rallies. And she's worked with Greenpeace militants and hired anti-oil activists . So it's no wonder that she's also against finding export routes for the oil we have, opposing both Keystone XL and Northern Gateway. We've already seen her plan for the oil industry: higher corporate taxes, higher taxes on emissions and higher royalty rates. Notley's idea of leading Canada's oil province is getting rid of the oil part. Unfortunately, she has nothing to replace it with.

So no wonder she appointed as her chief of staff an eastern anti-oil crusader named Brian Topp. He ran a campaign in B.C. aimed at blocking Alberta's pipelines. His team lost. He also wanted to be the leader of the federal NDP. We all know how that worked out. And he wants to ban vehicles from Canada's roads, because they burn fossil fuel. He actually said that. He compares Alberta's oil to weapons of mass destruction. He calls Alberta employers a "blight" on the Canadian economy. He thinks Canada needs to "produce a great deal less hydrocarbon energy." This is a peculiar idea, because we could freeze to death without hydrocarbon energy in our long, cold Alberta winters. If Mr. Topp ever bothered to move here permanently, he'd quickly find that out. He's now the most powerful man in Alberta's government apparatus.

Meanwhile, the minister actually in charge of energy, Margaret McCuaig-Boyd, won't be much help. She's actually a small-town teacher who came in way out of her depth. That's worrisome enough, but what's worse is that Topp hand picked the minister's chief of staff himself. That would be Graham Mitchell, who was the head of an American-funded lobby group that was committed to shutting down Alberta's oil production. The staffer now effectively running the energy ministry lobbied against the oil sands, against pipelines, against oil by rail, and he ran ads attacking Stephen Harper's government for being pro-oil. Oh, and in his spare time he worked as an activist coach, training more shock troops in the fight against fossil fuels. Let's hope Mitchell's free time was scarce. The world doesn't need another how-to book by the likes of Mike Hudema and Shannon Phillips.

And the man they all picked to head up the royalty panel that will determine the future of Alberta's oil industry? He did his own training — as a disciple of Al Gore. Dave Mowat, who is also head of Alberta Treasury Branches, was one of a select few people in the world picked by the global guru of anti-fossil-fuel campaigning to spread the global-warming religion of An Inconvenient Truth worldwide. But Mowat undoubtedly stands out as one of Gore's most promising pupils, as he's surely the only acolyte who will actually succeed in slamming the brakes on an entire province's oil sector. He'll do what other globe trotting Gore-bots have only dreamed of doing. He will shut it all down.

In a way, this book comes too late. The media, the other parties, and yes, the voters, all of us should have done a far better job scrutinizing Rachel Notley's team of radicals long before we let them anywhere near the corridors of power. Heck, even the NDP didn't vet Deborah Drever. Even after being elected, the NDP seems unbothered by the normal checks and balances of governing: Brian Topp continued working as a lobbyist even after he was appointed to government, somehow thinking it was okay to work for both sides of the street (it's actually a scandalous conflict of interest). Tony Clark, weeks after taking the job of chief of staff to the human services minister, was still registered as a union lobbyist, lobbying the very ministry that he's now running. And then there's Brent Dancey. He was appointed chief of staff to Shannon Phillips, who is also the minister responsible for the status of women. Turns out Dancey has a record — he was convicted of assault.

New Democrats are as discombobulated by their election as anyone. After a lifetime as a weak protest party, they never thought they'd actually be given power. That's why the Alberta NDP has attracted so many cranks over the years. It became the rest home for government-funded left-wing activists. It was historically the glue factory where the public-sector unions sent their old nags. This isn't Roy Romanow's Saskatchewan NDP — an at-least serious-minded party of realists with moderate ideas about running a province. Alberta's NDP is an out-of-touch tribe of lifelong ideological warriors. These are union activists, environmental radicals, socialists at best and Marxists if we are being honest. You'd look hard to find anyone in their caucus who actually thinks like a normal, everyday Albertan. Heck, some of the most powerful people in charge aren't even from Alberta.

Albertans have hitched a ride with a mad drunk. A drunk at the wheel of a garbage truck. That he's set on fire. And the ride is four years long. Oh, and you're paying for the booze and the gas. I wish I could say there was a way this will end well. It won't. When things get bad, when polls sink, the socialists will surely assume they're just not digging hard enough and fast enough, and they'll do it harder and faster. They think you voted for this. They think you want this. Throughout history, communists have always considered the cure for their man-made calamities to be more terrible communism. Double down. Triple down. And these guys know the clock is ticking; they'll need to hurry if they want to succeed in tearing down the things that hard-working, sensible Albertans took generations to build. They have one chance to get it all done.

So, yes, absolutely, we should have been more careful before electing these dangerous zealots. And we won't be complacent again. It's too late to be careful now. But the least we can do is be prepared. This book is an emergency survival manual that will at least help understand the enemy we're dealing with. We'll need all the intel we can get if we want to survive the onslaught that Rachel Notley's NDP government is about to unleash on Alberta.

CHAPTER 1

RACHEL NOTLEY

Wacky as this may sound, Alberta's premier, Rachel Notley, has a thing for Communist revolutionaries. Seriously. Sure, it's hard to believe. How could the 51-year-old premier of a staunchly free-enterprise province be that weird? In a country that stands tall on the world stage for freedom and democracy, and stood with the U.S. and Britain for decades against Communism, we have a premier with fondness for Communist guerrillas?

Sadly, yes. For years Notley has walked into Alberta's legislature — the seat of the province's democracy — wearing a wristwatch that has emblazoned on it the face of Che Guevara, the Argentinian Marxist guerrilla leader who played a key role in the Cuban communist revolution and served as a minister under Fidel Castro. He was also, like pretty much all Communist vanguard leaders, willing to murder anyone who stood in the way of the Communist cause.

Maybe she thinks it's just harmless. Che Guevara is known more as a fashionable image these days, his face more of a symbol for college kids who want to wear him on a T-shirt, or hang him on a dorm-room poster to signal some kind of rebelliousness against some kind of system. Or to impress girls and annoy their parents.

But those are kids. They're juvenile by definition. But Notley's old enough to be a grandmother, and she still hasn't grown out of her childish campus-style radicalism? She actually has such an attachment to the Communist icon that she'd wear it around on her person all day long, looking at it dozens of times a day whenever she wants to check the time. Imagine: Notley strutted around the halls of our democracy accessorizing her outfit with the image of someone who'd swiftly murder people for wanting a democracy such as ours. It's callous at best. Thomas Lukaszuk, a PC MLA in the legislature with Notley and whose family defected from Communist Poland, said he even tried to tell her how "hurtful it is" for her to glorify one of the darlings of a system that brutally oppressed and murdered so many millions. Evidently, she was okay with that. It matches her shoes.

So this is the woman who Albertans have handed control of their economically vital province over to. It's pretty clear they didn't know what they were getting. Because Rachel Notley isn't just a regular old Albertan whose defining political characteristic is that she's not an old-boy PC. We have a lot of those, already. She's an old-school socialist, a Bernie Sanders in a bob haircut. She's a crusader for the labour union movement — her husband, Lou Arab, is the communications officer for the Canadian Union of Public Employees. His Twitter account disappeared at the onset of her election campaign. Very convenient. Arab's far-left union appears to have even merged with the government since Notley took office: Once, when CBC reporters called Arab's phone number, given out to media on a CUPE press release, bizarrely, it was the premier's press secretary who returned the call.

This is the same CUPE, by the way, that has campaigned against Canada's fight against the Islamic State; who cheered the efforts of Greece's far-left prime minister Alex Tsipras to spurn Greece's debts; who accuses Israel, of "unjust and disproportionate violence" in its defense against rocket attacks from Gaza. Hey — given the family's devotion to violent revolutionary guerrillas, maybe Notley's husband has a matching Yassir Arafat watch.

But while Notley seems to enjoy accessorizing with the image of a man who was considered the "executioner-in-chief" of the Cuban revolution's class enemies, she's got a real problem with Alberta's oil and gas producers. She has warned that "unfettered development" of the oil sands is bad for the province; she would rather that investment and development and jobs be, well, fettered.

Slow down the expansion," she has said, until oil sands companies clean up their environmental act. She specifically has an issue with tailings ponds, the focus of so much anti-oil sands propaganda. Now, tailings ponds exist all across Canada, used for decades by mining operations from B.C. to Newfoundland. But Notley sticks to campaigning against the Albertan ones. She likes to call them "toxic tailings lakes," to make them sound that much worse. When the Premier could be celebrating our homegrown achievements with regard to tailings and land reclamation as the global benchmark for success, Notley downplays the good — sort of like she does with capitalism. Notley and her comrades, Brian Topp, Infrastructure Minister Brian Mason, Education Minister Dave Eggen, and energy staff chief Graeme Mitchell, insist on still using the term "tar sands," to make the oil sound that much dirtier.

Notley has campaigned for years against her despised "toxic lakes" (in reality, these man-made reservoirs are made up largely of water being separated from sand and clay; because the water also has some traces of oil left in it, it would be toxic to fish — if someone were foolish enough to drop some fish into them). The ponds are supposed to have deterrents that keep waterfowl away, so they don't get stuck in the oil that can collect on the surface: scarecrows and noise cannons, for instance. There have been a few cases where those have failed, and ducks have unfortunately died.

No one likes that. But this was no duck holocaust. The company responsible, Syncrude, was fined $3 million. But that didn't satiate Notley's revenge lust for those doomed waterfowl. Notley has called it a "tragedy" that "represents ... a great deal of pain and suffering to the ducks, but also it represents the inherent conflict that exists between unbridled industrial growth that is conflicted with environmental protection, health protection and community protection." Ducks. Not Donald. Not Scrooge McDuck. Not even those pesky duck nephews. Such drama for some unfortunate random ducks. Imagine if geese had died that fateful day. Notley would still be wearing black. She has said that the oil sands have "poisoned" fish populations. Where, though, I'm not sure. No matter what anyone says nowadays, Rachel Notley has never been pro-oil sands. Not now, not ever.

Notice the pattern of her demands: decrying the oil sands' so-called "unfettered development"; "their "unbridled" growth; calling for oil sands growth to "slow down." It's pretty clear what she's saying: Don't expect an NDP government to start granting new approvals for oil sands projects. And why would we? Notley spent her career, before she was elected, representing the anti-oil constituency in the legislature.

And let's just examine the accuracy of that statement: unfettered development. Many oil sands projects see years and years of stagnation in the onerous and often redundant approval process in Alberta. It's long been part of Alberta's commitment to being a good environmental and community steward. Notley knows this. She can't not know this. She's a lifelong Alberta politician and the daughter of a lifelong Alberta politician. But it's important to her movement, her narrative and her agenda to have the unwitting public think it's the Wild West out here. It's just cowboys in white Hank Williams suits shooting pistols in the air when an oil company drills another gusher, or so Notley would have you believe.

Just a little while before she became premier, she actually attended a rally where protesters carried signs reading "no tar sands, no tankers, no pipelines." In September, she appointed a B.C. anti-pipeline activist, Marcella Munro, to run the premier's office in Calgary — Canada's oil-company capital. And when Notley was in opposition, one of her staffers was a Greenpeace activist, who stormed into a dinner being held for the premier to protest against government support for the oil industry. Notley also employed professional protester and one-time NDP candidate Mike Hudema as a legislative staffer. He's the co-author of that how-to-be-a-radical manual with Shannon Phillips. He took that social justice lawlessness he wrote about to heart. He was part of the Occupy Edmonton group of trespassers and once chained himself to the Shell Scotford upgrader.

Notley has come out and said that now that she's premier she'll hand the decision over whether we should build the Energy East pipeline — from Alberta to refineries in New Brunswick — to the Liberal governments in Ontario and Quebec, based on whether they think Alberta's doing enough to help fight climate change. She has said she wants to put the brakes on hydraulic fracturing of shale, or fracking — even though we've been doing it in Alberta for decades — now. She accuses the oil industry of "contaminating the water supply" and says that the government has "failed abysmally" in monitoring the industry's environmental impact. But Alberta's monitoring of the oil industry is actually among the most stringent in the world; does anyone think Russia or Rod Loyola's beloved Venezuela or Iran have stricter environmental controls? No other jurisdiction spends as much on environmental monitoring and remediation as Alberta does. But Notley is embarrassed of her province. Her schtick in opposition has always been shaming Alberta in front of Canada. And the world.

Understandably, Notley has lately been trying to cover up the fact that she's hostile to oil, trying to make it sound like she supports Alberta's oil industry. She has to keep up the charade. She's already bleeding support. But it's not hard to see that her heart isn't really in it. She's a left-wing, NDP eco-warrior through and through. That's why she surrounds herself with people from the radical anti-oil activist movements. It's not a coincidence: people like the energy ministry chief, Graham Mitchell, who actually headed up an anti-oil sands group, and Notley's own chief of staff, Brian Topp, who wants to ban fossil fuel and cars in urban areas. These are her kind of people: anti-oil radicals in smart shoes.

Left to right: Joe Ceci, David Eggen, Rachel Notley, and Shannon Phillips

And of course, her first priorities as premier were all about whacking the oilpatch: higher corporate taxes, doubling the emissions tax, and beginning a review to raise oil royalties, even though Albertans just had one a few years ago. It's all sold under the guise of Albertans getting and paying their fair share. She even raised personal taxes on "the wealthy," which in Alberta, let's face it, means people in the oilpatch — even middle-class ones. In Fort McMurray, Alberta's oil sands epicentre, the average household income is higher than Notley's $125,000 "wealthy" income threshold.

The premier is also against building any new pipelines for Alberta crude. That's an astonishing thing, when you think about it. She actually opposes Keystone XL and Northern Gateway — two pipelines that would allow the producers in her province to sell more of their product, invest more money, create more jobs. Even though both of those pipelines have been given approval by the federal energy regulator. She's still against those export proposals. For the leader of an oil-producing province, it's a position that's remarkably hostile to the oil sector.

It's like the premier of Ontario coming out against exporting too many auto parts.

Notley tries to cover up her position by making it sound like she has better ideas for what to do with all our oil — better ideas than what the industry and investors who have been doing this for decades think should be done. She claims that the Keystone XL pipeline to the U.S. Gulf Coast would be bad for Alberta because it would take jobs away from the province. "If we ship unprocessed bitumen to Texas ... we will give tens of thousands of Alberta jobs to Texans," she told the legislature this summer, trying to explain away her opposition to Keystone XL. But that's a nonsensical argument: Virtually every single job in Alberta's oil industry exists precisely because we export unprocessed oil. Exporting oil is what we've been doing for half a century. We ship millions of barrels to the U.S. every single day. That's our industry; it's what has made Alberta the richest province in the entire country. And now we have a premier who is suddenly against it? A premier who wants to prevent any more of it?

Notley wraps her logic in the claim that Alberta needs to build projects to refine oil, too — because that would create more jobs. It's actually not true: what creates jobs is investors putting their capital to work as efficiently as they can. And we need to sell the product in the form our one and only foreign customer, the U.S., wants it in. Our customer has their own under-capacity refineries. It's like arguing that Alberta farmers shouldn't be allowed to sell their wheat to export markets, but should be forced to bake it into bread, first.

There's a reason investors aren't building refineries in Alberta; they don't see it as an economical use of the money they invest here. Losing money on a refinery isn't going to help anybody create many long-lasting jobs. Let's, just for argument's sake, disregard that we already have more than enough refining capacity and that the Heartland Region region already does 75 percent of the refining and upgrading in western Canada. Even if someone did want to build another refinery, that would take years, perhaps a decade. Is Notley saying we should just cancel any additional exports until then? Keep the oil in the ground? Is that her plan to "slow down" the oil sands? Because that's certainly one way to do it.

In fact, you'll notice that all of Notley's plans for the oil industry have one thing in common. The higher taxes, the steeper royalties, tougher emissions penalties, putting a halt on fracking approvals, blocking new oil sands approvals, handing climate vetoes to other provinces, opposing new pipelines: they're all aimed at demolishing Alberta's oil and gas industry. It's a soft revolution of economic disincentives. That's Alberta's new revolutionary leader.

CHAPTER 2

BRIAN TOPP

I n 2013, B.C.'s NDP leader Adrian Dix ran for premier and promised he would allow no more pipelines transferring oil from Alberta to the coast. None. Certainly not Northern Gateway, the proposed pipeline that would allow Alberta oil to find its way to the biggest tankers in the deep waters of B.C.'s northwest coast. But Dix also said he would block the expansion of an existing pipeline, Kinder Morgan's Trans Mountain pipeline, which delivers 300,000 barrels of Alberta oil to the Vancouver suburb of Burnaby, B.C. and has been moving oil safely since 1953. Vancouver, he said, was not interested in becoming an "oil export port" for Alberta's most important product. He's 62 years too late to be taking that position. In fact, he said, the entire province was off limits to more oil from Alberta.

Dix lost that election in brutal fashion. Even British Columbians were stunned by the fantasy idealism that Canada should just lock up its oil inside Alberta's borders and figure out some other business to be in.

But westerners are realistic like that. And the campaign manager running Dix's campaign was no realist. And he was no westerner.

He was Brian Topp.

Topp is a union leader and NDP executive from Ontario. He could hardly be less Albertan: he actually supports bringing back the long-gun registry, arguing that its only flaw was that it previously cost too much — not that it treated average, law-abiding hunters and sports shooters like criminals. He was one of the masterminds behind an anti-Harper coalition between the NDP, the Liberals and the separatist Bloc Québécois that would have brought down a Conservative government elected in large part by western support. He's not one of us. Frankly, he's against those things we hold dear in the west.

But Topp hops on a plane and flies out west whenever there's an opportunity to fight against Alberta's oil industry. And on May 12, 2015, Brian Topp was headed west again. That's because he was hired as the chief of staff to the premier of Alberta.

That's right: the guy who wanted to create a B.C. boycott against Albertan oil exports is the man that premier Rachel Notley picked to be the most powerful executive in the provincial government.

Don't assume Topp is just a political gun for hire. He wasn't strategizing for Dix's B.C. campaign because he's a mercenary, and he didn't just come here because he's getting paid more than $200,000 a year to run Notley's government. Topp surely makes more than that as a lobbyist, which may be why he was still registered as a lobbyist until June, weeks after his appointment to Notley's office (he finally resigned — only after he was publicly outed for the egregious conflict of interest).

So this isn't Topp being opportunistic. This is his life's work coming to fruition. Taking the helm of the Alberta government is the culminating moment in a campaign he's been fighting since as far back as he's been a prominent political operator. It's a chance to drastically uproot Alberta's entire economy from the inside. Because, Brian Topp actually hates Alberta oil.

He's anti-pipeline. He's anti-oil sands. He's anti-coal. He's anti every fossil fuel that comes out of Alberta's sediment.

We already saw his anti-pipeline colours in the Dix campaign. But even years before that, Topp made no secret about his opposition to piping out Alberta oil. **In 2011, he told the Vancouver-area Georgia Straight newspaper** that he's dead-set against the proposed Keystone XL pipeline, too. That's the line from Alberta to the U.S. Gulf that TransCanada tried to get President Barack Obama to approve for eight years and that he finally rejected in November, even though it was repeatedly cleared by both Obama's own State Department and the Environmental Protection Agency as having no problematic environmental impact. That line doesn't cross B.C. It doesn't go anywhere near Brian Topp's house several provinces to the east. But he's against it because, well, it's a pipeline that helps

Alberta's energy economy. To Topp, that's economic "madness" — that's what he called it.

Topp was even careful to make sure the reporter had no doubt whatsoever about what his vision was: "... let's be clear, I think it should be stopped," he said of Keystone. "It is a fundamentally wrong economic choice and a wrong environmental choice with enormous consequences on the streets of Vancouver and all across the country." Except, Keystone goes nowhere near the "streets of Vancouver." Topp knows that. What he means is that anti-oil extremists outside Alberta, like him, don't like it. But what about on the "streets" of Fort McMurray, one of the cities that Brian Topp is now tasked with helping to govern? Or on the streets of little Hardisty, where the first pumping station of Keystone waited in hope of work? Or on the streets of Edmonton? Or in Calgary, where the office towers downtown sit half full? Topp never cared about the livelihoods of the oil and gas workers who live on those streets before. Don't think for a minute that he suddenly cares about them now.

In fact, Topp sees Alberta as a province that needs to be shown the error of its ways. He's said as much. The first step in stopping Keystone, he told the same reporter, was to "win the battle of ideas in Alberta." He actually plans to convince Albertans that, no, we don't really want to sell all that oil and gas we produce. Oh, and we don't want those well-paying jobs. We just need convincing.

But wait a minute. Did the NDP win a "battle of ideas" in Alberta that would give Topp licence to just suddenly turn around a provincial policy that has been pro-Keystone, and other pipelines? Of course not. We know that for a fact. **As the crucial survey of Albertan voters** after the election by Abacus Data showed, 93 percent of Albertans say the election of the NDP was about a desire for change — a "throw-the-bums-out" fit, after Jim Prentice's Tories pulled a few too many fast ones. Only seven percent — seven! — said the vote had anything to do with a preference for the NDP. Even the overwhelming majority of NDP voters admitted it wasn't because people suddenly fell in love with their party's ideas. They didn't even know the NDP's ideas, let alone the rag-tag bunch of candidates the NDP fielded. They didn't even really grow all that fond of Notley herself: two-thirds of respondents say the result was more about "cooling on Jim Prentice" rather than "warming to Rachel Notley." Voters saw her as the best worst option between the entitlement of the PCs and the disarray of the Wildrose.

Remember, Topp isn't from Alberta. He doesn't know Alberta and he doesn't really want to. He thinks like an easterner. He ran Adrian Dix's campaign in B.C., a western, resource-based economy, by vilifying resources, and ended up handing Christy Clark a stronger majority than she had before, even though most political observers figured she was toast. He didn't know B.C. either. So when he sees an NDP victory in Alberta, he could very well think that suddenly Alberta is coming around to his way of seeing the world. And his way of seeing the world is to make sure that Keystone — and all of Alberta's oil exports in every other pipeline — are stopped.

Because he's not just against selling our oil, he's against producing it, too. He told that Georgia Straight reporter that he thinks the oil sands have a "shocking" impact on the environment and said that Canada "should produce a great deal less hydrocarbon energy." Of course what that means is that, the way he sees it, Albertans need to be a "great deal less" employed. And colder.

That's not an exaggeration: Topp has been upfront about the fact that he thinks Canada needs to end its economic focus on resource energy. He's even said the pro-energy policies of the Alberta and federal governments are "blighting the rest of our economy." That all the social services and health care that Alberta's resource revenues pay for here at home, and across the country through billions in equalization payments, are immoral. Our governments are "taxing their grandchildren through a resource rip-off," he said. Three pipelines alone — Keystone XL, Northern Gateway and Trans Mountain — according to the Canadian Export Pipeline Association, would contribute almost one and a half trillion dollars to the Canadian GDP over the next 25 years. This is what Brian Topp calls a blight on the economy.

His solution, predictably, is drying up the resource industry and paying for these things instead through higher income taxes. That's hardly surprising: Topp is a socialist — he represented the NDP at **Socialist International meetings** in Europe.

He even threw his **support** behind the anti-capitalist Occupy movement, like Notley and her husband Lou Arab did. And he's said that he sees income tax as a tool to "**redistribute**" wealth among the public. He believes in higher corporate taxes. And he's said he wants to raise taxes for "high-income earners." Of course, in Alberta, his definition of a "high income" may well end up sweeping up those families struggling to afford the basic living expenses of an oil town like Fort McMurray. There, **the average household income** is well into six-figures a year, but food and housing cost 50 percent more than the Alberta average.

When Topp was running against Thomas Mulcair for the leadership of the federal NDP, he lost because he was considered too far left, even for party supporters who once rallied behind Jack Layton. During one leadership debate, he actually pledged to force "fossil-fuelled cars out of our cities." That was no gaffe. Topp is firmly committed to completely overhauling the Canadian economy, getting it out of oil and gas and into expensive solar power and wind farms. In his very own platform for the NDP leadership, he vowed to "Develop a national energy strategy to transition Canada to a low-carbon economy and limit the impacts of oil sands development during the transition."

Topp wouldn't even agree, when asked by The Globe and Mail, that since the world was going to use oil anyway, perhaps it would be better that as much of it as possible should be ethical Canadian oil. After all, the world's demand for oil has only gotten bigger, with people consuming right now about 90 million barrels a day, and the appetite is growing. And unlike Iran, or Russia, or Venezuela, or Nigeria, Canada is a democracy with a pristine human rights record, doesn't threaten its neighbours, gives rights to workers, and treats minorities and women as equals. Plus, we produce oil with an environmental record that's as stringent and successful as anyone's. We are the global benchmark for good resource extraction practices.

But Topp doesn't care. To him, oil is the enemy. It's a weapon of mass destruction. Seriously, that's how he responded. "We're a nice democracy," he mocked. "So any product we produce is 'ethical' … Let's get into ethical landmines." How very clever. Topp actually compared our peaceful production of products that every single one of us uses every day — that we need to use every day to power our homes, businesses and our schools and hospitals — to making weapons of murder. What an insult to the thousands of men and women who work every day to bring Alberta's oil to market, safely. Apparently, they may as well be planting bombs in the road. How committed will Alberta's new top government boss be to ensuring the successful development and export of something he judges to be so wicked, so immoral and so deadly?

You don't need to wait to find out. Topp has already said he considers the lack of action in reducing greenhouse gases to be one of Canada's "greatest failures." He's actually protested efforts made by the Alberta government and the oil industry to counter international efforts to blacklist Alberta oil as especially "dirty," as activist legislators in California and the European Union have done. He campaigned against Canada and against Alberta, against our jobs and our workers. And he's argued for a "legally binding ban on oil tankers" off the northwest coast of B.C. — one of the few outlets that Alberta would have to ship its oil to overseas markets. He wants to landlock our oil.

Topp is also a fan of policies like "what they're doing in Europe," he says, which he says includes: "a hard cap on emissions, to price carbon, a home and industrial retrofit program, getting out of coal, getting an urban mass-transit program, and getting fossil-fuelled cars out of our cities." That, he said, has "got to be at the heart" of government policy here.

If Topp likes "what they're doing in Europe" that may be because Europe doesn't rely on a resource-based economy the way we do here in Canada, and especially in Alberta. "Getting out of coal" for heaven's sake? More than **40 percent** of Alberta's power comes from coal. Only a fraction comes from non-fossil-fuel energy. There isn't much hydro power in Alberta, and there is no nuclear power. So Topp either plans to pull the plug on nearly half of Alberta's electrical grid, or, more likely, he plans to turn the province into another experiment in expensive green energy. In Germany's crusade to switch its grid to "green" sources, the average electricity bill paid by businesses has **jumped 60 percent**, drastically impacting that country's economic competitiveness. A stubborn renewables push in Spain has helped drive electricity bills for consumers to **among the highest** in Europe. Is that the European model Topp has in mind for Alberta?

And really, we don't have to look that far to see the damage that a drastic shift to green energy can have. Let's look to Ontario. They made a drastic jump to green energy and Ontarians saw an immediate 40 percent jump in their power rates. Those hikes in rates are predicted to continue. This is what Brian Topp has in store for Albertans: energy poverty.

And then there's that "hard cap" on emissions. There's no question that Alberta has higher greenhouse gas emissions than any other province. There's a reason for that: we produce the energy here that is then sent across the country. In other words, Canadians — and a lot of Americans — park their emissions here in Alberta, so they can have the energy they need to live, move and work. It's called wells to wheels measurements, and it means the end user's carbon output is attributed to the producer. Putting a "hard cap" on that really means putting a "hard cap" on the growth of Alberta's primary industry. It means no new projects. It means no new jobs. In fact, it means fewer of the jobs we already have.

And there really is no major urban centre in Europe that has gotten "fossil-fuelled cars" entirely out of the city (merely a few confined car-free historic and pedestrian areas, just as there are in Canada). But that embellished fantasy tells you everything you need to know about how Topp thinks and how little he knows about Alberta. We aren't downtown Toronto. We use cars and trucks to get around. His ultimate goal is to see the end of fossil fuels. Of course that would also mean an effective end to Alberta's economy. Incredibly, Brian Topp has just become the most well-placed man in the entire country with the will and the power to help that come to pass.

CHAPTER 3

GRAHAM MITCHELL

N ot long ago a far-left environmentalist orga-
nization called LeadNow released an attack
ad that aimed its barrels at two targets. The first
target: Conservatives. The second: Alberta's oil and
gas industry.

"The Harper government has stripped out our
environmental protections, put all our economic
eggs in one risky (resource) basket, and damaged
our international reputation. They've taken our
country backwards," the narrator says, as the video
shows crude black oil being spilled over forests and
rivers, with the words "TAR SANDS," "PIPELINES"
and "SUBSIDIES TO OIL AND GAS" flashed on the
screen in dark tones.

Obviously whoever devised that ad sure hates
Alberta's oil and gas industry — not to mention Stephen Harper, the former prime minister from Alberta.

Meet Graham Mitchell, the new chief of staff to
Alberta's energy minister. You heard that right: the
man who was running LeadNow — a group fund-
ed by the powerfully anti-oil sands Tides Foundation — right up until the NDP took power, is now in
charge of running Alberta's energy department.

Of course, Graham Mitchell isn't from Alberta. He wasn't born here and hasn't been living here. Like so many top-ranking NDP government leaders, he parachuted in from his home in Toronto. But Mitchell surely ranks as one of the most explicitly anti-Albertan power players running this province now. Two days before Notley appointed him to take the helm of the energy ministry, he was still working as a hard-core anti-oil lobbyist — he was actually registered with the federal lobbying commissioner as professionally working to lobby on tighter restrictions for the oil sands, shipping oil by rail car, carbon emissions, and pipelines. He was also lobbying against trade deals for exporting Canadian goods.

That means that just days before his hiring, Albertans were getting up in the morning to go to work producing energy for the provincial economy, and Graham Mitchell was getting up to go work in Ottawa to put Alberta's energy workers out of a job. Now he's actually got the keys to the ministry that controls the fate of those jobs. Radical environmentalists hardly need to bother lobbying against Alberta's oil industry anymore; they have their own guy ready to dismantle it from the inside.

Because, make no mistake: it's bad enough that Mitchell was working as executive director of LeadNow, whose campaigns run the narrow gamut from agitating against pipelines, to pushing for higher taxes on the oil industry, to fighting against the shipment of oil by rail, to advocating for stricter carbon-emission rules. But Mitchell's far-left activism has been a lifelong passion. He was executive assistant to Jack Layton back when Layton was the most far-left city councillor in Toronto. He supported Olivia Chow, Layton's widow and socialist candidate for Toronto mayor in the city's 2014 election. And after Chow lost, Mitchell decided it was because she wasn't nearly militant enough in her radicalism. As he wrote on Twitter: "@oliviachow movement advice: stop being nice and DEMAND more. Work together - some negotiate and others demand. Be creative." That was a bit of a switch for Mitchell, who often uses his Twitter feed to promote articles from environmentalist websites going after the government's dealings with what he refers to scornfully as "Big Oil" and to share stories about the "inspiring" work of activists who work to ban natural gas fracking.

Up until he was hired to run Alberta's energy ministry staff, he was also a director at the federal NDP think tank, the Broadbent Institute, where he actually trained other lefty activists to campaign against oil and gas. He's trained them to fight for bans against gas fracking. Fracking is as Albertan as wheat fields and cowboys, being done safely here for five decades. When it comes to hating Alberta oil and gas, Graham Mitchell is like an environmentalist Tony Robbins, inspiring an army of young, energetic revolutionaries to Awaken the Oil-Denouncing Giant Within. He's the archduke of anti-oil activism. Putting Graham Mitchell in charge of the energy department is as crazy as appointing the head of PETA to be the agriculture minister. Crazy, that is, unless your goal is to undermine Alberta's energy economy.

Which is surely exactly why Mitchell got his job. Even though he's chief of staff to the energy minister, Margaret McCuaig-Boyd, she didn't actually hire him. As a minister's chief of staff, he was hired by the premier's chief of staff: Brian Topp, another oil hater from the east. It's even become clear that Margaret McCuaig-Boyd had no idea that she was being given a radical anti-Albertan to run her department. When news broke about Mitchell's background, and reporters at the legislature confronted her about it, she found herself at a loss to explain it as reporters pressed McCuaig-Boyd repeatedly to answer how someone who has dedicated his career to anti-oil activism could possibly look like the right choice to preside over the energy ministry. She plainly had no idea what she'd been ambushed with. "I understand he worked for LeadNow or whatever it's called," she said. She said she needed to get more "details" about it. She, like the rest of us, had suddenly found herself being screwed over by the Ontario-headquartered anti-Alberta junta.

McCuaig-Boyd certainly doesn't seem like a radical anti-oil sands activist herself. She actually hails from Alberta, not the activist drum-circles of Queen St. East. She's a small-town teacher from

Fairview, which makes her a weird choice to run Alberta's most important economic file. But at least she's about as normal as NDPers get. She's probably one of most typically Albertan people in Rachel Notley's cabinet. And there's no apparent reason to doubt it when she says, as she has, that she wants to work with the oil and gas industry. Who knows? McCuaig-Boyd might even have the potential to be a moderating force against some of the raving NDP radicals around her in this government.

But she can't really be that, if her department is being overseen by a non-Albertan anti-oil lobbyist who was put there by another non-Albertan ant-oil lobbyist — Brian Topp, himself the most powerful political staffer in the government.

Because, let's be realistic: Alberta's energy economy is a mind-bogglingly complex thing. It isn't for amateurs. The minister has already acknowledged the royalty system as "**complicated**" (which it kind of has to be, when you're dealing with an industry that encompasses old wells, revitalized wells, entirely new wells, gas production, fracking, gas pipelines, oil pipelines, upgrading, oil sands mining, oil sands steaming (SAGD), bitumen swapping, various world market prices for various kinds of oil and gas, currency fluctuations, and much more).

Have sympathy for McCuaig-Boyd. She's been given a brutally tricky file that only has implications for, oh, about a third or more of the provincial economy. In a field this technical, it would probably take her or any non-expert months just to develop the vocabulary to capably sit down and talk about things like dilbit and blow-downs, or fugitive emissions, orphaned wells or proppants.

In fact, Graham Mitchell probably knows a lot more going in about the oil and gas industry than his own minister does. But not in a practical sense, not in any way that reflects the good work Albertans do every day. Mitchell knows he wants to end it all. And that is surely why Brian Topp put him there. Mitchell knows what he's doing, even if McCuaig-Boyd is still trying to figure out the basic "details" of the man running her staff. And what Mitchell is doing is making sure that everything he had to try lobbying for in Ottawa is going to become Alberta government policy. The rejection of pipelines; putting the brakes on oil shipment by rail; stopping approvals of new projects ; silencing the voice of "Big Oil," as he calls it.

As chief of staff, he gets to handle what speeches the minister gives and he gets to decide who the minister meets with. How likely do you think it is we'll be hearing speeches offering a full-throated defence of Alberta's energy exports, given that Mitchell has personally fought to keep Alberta oil landlocked? How much room do you think he'll be making in the minister's calendar to hear from representatives of Alberta's vital energy industry, given that he's actually worked to shut "Big Oil" out of government decision-making processes?

As chief of staff to the energy minister, Graham Mitchell will have his hands on the levers of the energy department's powerful machinery. Historically that machinery was used to promote Alberta's best economic interests. With Mitchell at the controls, an anti-oil activist just visiting the province, picture instead a bulldozer.

CHAPTER 4

ROD LOYOLA

Albertans are sometimes known to kid around about the NDP being a bunch of "commies" — lefties who love big government and high taxes and sometimes fantasize about nationalizing key industries. But usually we assume — or maybe we just hope — that we're exaggerating at least a little bit. Sure, Rachel Notley wears that bizarre Che Guevara wristwatch. But we don't exactly picture her quoting Mao's Little Red Book or singing along to The Internationale.

But then, Albertans haven't quite gotten to know Rod Loyola. At least not yet.

Rod Loyola — or, Rodrigo Alonso Loyola Salas, his actual name — is the elected NDP member for the riding of Edmonton–Ellerslie. He came to Alberta from Chile, where he was born during the Marxist presidency of Salvador Allende.

It must have stuck. Because Loyola is also a Communist. To be clear, we're not talking about a socialist here, with the Scandinavian sensibilities that are so common in the NDP and Liberal parties. Nor is Loyola just some callow college kid who gets a kick out of reading Marx and dressing in guerilla-chic Sandinista fatigues. No, he's an actual

47

Communist. As in, the real, red deal. The full hammer-and-sickle situation.

loyola has praised the Communist model of Cuba, and **defends its government** as "democratic." He talks about the "lumpenproletariat" — Marx's term for those in the working class who are useless to the revolutionary struggle. The lumpenproletariat is the oilpatch in Alberta. Fully dispensable to NDPers like Loyola. Loyola isn't in the "working class" himself, really: he's been a union leader; but that was on a university campus. When he wanted to get to know the experience of actual oil and gas workers, he went to — get this — **a museum**: the Leduc #1 Discovery Centre, near Edmonton, which he said gave him "a whole new appreciation for workers on an oil drill" (presumably he meant an oil rig). The experience has changed, just a bit, since Leduc #1 blew in on February 13, 1947.

But Loyola is so committed to the Communist cause that he has stood before crowds to praise the late Venezuelan strongman Hugo Chávez and his disastrous "Bolivarian revolution" that turned that rich country into a corrupt Marxist economic ruin. "Long live Hugo Chávez. Long live the values that he stood for," Loyola says in a video that **he hosted on his YouTube channel** (he's since tried to block it). "Compañero Presidente Hugo Chávez!" (meaning: "comrade president Hugo Chávez!") he booms, as his fellow Communists chant more praise for the "revolutionary" leader back at him. When Chávez died in 2013, Loyola organized a vigil for him, **calling it** "an opportunity to express solidarity with the Venezuelan people and support for the Bolivarian Revolution" and to "share with the media and local community the hard work, dedication and achievements of President Hugo Chávez and his government." Last year, Loyola wrote on his Facebook page that Canada could learn a lot from Chávez's authoritarian leadership: "especially regarding democracy and social and economic justice."

Is that so? Before Chávez died, he had already racked up a long rap sheet with human rights groups like Amnesty International and Human Rights Watch. Chávez ruthlessly persecuted any dissent against his demented Bolivarian Revolution, drawing up laws stifling free speech that threatened journalists accused of "media crimes" with imprisonment. He cracked down on labour unions, which he saw as a threat to his power. His regime rounded up and arrested political activists, it harassed and illegally detained human rights activists championing indigenous land rights for Venezuela's native Yupka aboriginals. Dissidents were killed.

Even Chávez's death, his disastrous communist legacy continues to ruin Venezuela, where **inflation has gotten so out of control** that it's now the highest in the world, and where there are desperate shortages of food and other supplies. Certainly in his home country, Chávez's legacy hasn't remained quite as pristine as it seems to be in Loyola's mind.

And one of the late authoritarian leader's first steps toward sowing all this calamity was when he began **seizing and nationalizing oil assets**.

It should be no surprise then that one of the most urgent priorities of Chávez's No. 1 Canadian fanboy, Rod Loyola, now that he's in an NDP government, is to start bringing the Alberta government down hard — very hard — on the oil industry.

loyola once actually tried to become the leader of the provincial NDP, enticed perhaps to try for himself the commanding authoritarian heights achieved by Dear Leader Comrade Chávez. In 2014, he ran against Rachel Notley to head up the party. Notley ended up winning with 70 percent party support. Loyola managed two percent.

During the campaign, Loyola sat down for **an interview** with the Alberta Teachers' Association to talk about his education policies. But Loyola couldn't resist using the opportunity to talk about his plan for squeezing the oil companies, to fund "education, and health care and every other social program that we needed to in this province." Now, most Albertans know that the province is already one of the biggest spenders per capita on health care and education in the entire country. And that Alberta's spending is already largely paid for by royalties from oil and gas. But that's not nearly good enough for Loyola. He said it's "absolutely essential [we're] making sure that oil royalties are a lot higher than what they actually are right now. And I would even say that we need to get them to at least thirty, thirty-five percent..."

Royalties in Alberta average about nine percent right now. And notice how Loyola says at least 30 or 35 percent. For Loyola, more than tripling royalties is an absolute minimum. But really, he wants to hit Alberta's energy industry much, much harder. How much harder? Just last year he told The Leduc Rep newspaper that royalties should climb **as high as 60 percent**. That's nearly seven times higher than royalties are now — and it's higher than the **royalty rate in China**. It's even higher than the royalty rate in Venezuela, where Hugo Chávez practically nationalized the entire energy sector. But even that might not be high enough: A few years earlier, Loyola spoke to the People's Voice, a Communist magazine that ran an interview with him under his **hip-hop/slam poetry stage name** "Rosouljah" (he likes to rap about being a gun-toting gangster fighting against capitalism. Funny that, because the NDP oppose gun ownership). Loyola — er, sorry, Rosouljah — said "When a country like Venezuela gets over 80 percent of its petroleum back — for us this is a foretelling of a socialist future to come. Bolivia, Venezuela, Ecuador, Cuba: they all want more for their people."

And Loyola has a problem with Alberta oil companies especially: he sees them as colonial oppressors. In June 2014, **he told Edmonton's VUE Weekly magazine** that the "capitalism" of Alberta's resource industry is really the "colonization" of indigenous people. He compared the "corporate rule and neoliberalism" that he claims has happened in Alberta to military juntas that have seized power in Latin America, where he's from. "Essentially we're talking about communities that are trying to defend themselves from these economic systems and the oppression that those economic systems have created," Loyola said.

So, to Loyola, the Alberta energy sector represents "oppression." Not a jobs creator and generous employer of aboriginals in their own communities. No. To Loyola, the energy sector is a piñata to be bashed harder and harder until he's knocked out all the money he wants to fund any pricey new social-spending programs that his Bolivarian NDP revolution deems appropriate. According to Loyola, Alberta oil companies are colonial boogey men, yet he ignores what Chávez had done to the Yupka. There's that Lumpenproletariat again. Remember how Loyola said long live the values that Hugo Chávez stood for? Even he can't have possibly dreamt of a day that we'd all see them influencing the policies of Alberta's government.

But even Venezuela exports oil, some of it to Canada. That's the part of the Bolivarian revolution that Loyola left out.

CHAPTER 5

SHANNON PHILLIPS

"A democratic society doesn't just condone political action," writes Shannon Phillips with Mike Hudema in the introduction to their 2004 book An Action a Day Keeps Global Capitalism Away. "It demands it."

Here's a few of the anti-capitalist political actions that our society "demands," that they list off: "... it could be a roadside blockade"; "it might be the tens of thousands of people who moved into Quebec City ... to protest the Summit of the Americas"; "political action includes Greenpeace militants climbing to the top of a building to drop a banner."

Mike Hudema really is one of those militant Greenpeace activists — if you've followed the anti-oil debate at all in Alberta over the past 15 years, you've heard from Hudema.

And Shannon Phillips, the co-author of those words in the book about blockades and lawbreaking in the fight to keep "capitalism away"? She's your new environment minister.

Now that she's in politics, Phillips insists she doesn't endorse the entire book. She's distanced herself from some of the recommended chants referring to the oil industry as "genocide." **She does ad-**

mit it's a "radical" book. But she now says that she merely helped with "some grammar." All that credit Hudema gave her in the preface — how it would "not have been possible to put this book together without" Phillips, because "she pushed me to write it, edited my work and contributed to the content"? He's exaggerating, Phillips now says. Mike Hudema has a way of being "effusive," she said. Yep. Good ol' effusive Mike. The guy who **called Stephen Harper's legacy** a "a trail of destruction from gutting environmental safeguards, to pushing pipelines and tar sands projects regardless of the damage to the land, water, climate, community health or First Nations rights."

So before you go ascribing all the book's radical anti-capitalist ideas to Shannon Phillips, think twice. Because Shannon Phillips, or as she's known on her roller-derby team, **Gnome Stompsky** (named after the anarcho-communist MIT intellectual Noam Chomsky), has radical ideas all her own.

like how Alberta's oil industry is hurting women.

You might not think so. After all, women earn far **higher incomes** in Alberta than any other province and have better workforce participation rates. That doesn't sound very hurtful. The **divorce rate** in Alberta isn't unusually high or low, so women seem to be happily married as much as anywhere. The **life expectancy for women in Alberta** is second only to the first-place tie between B.C. and Ontario. The mayor of Fort McMurray's a woman. The premier's a woman. Alberta's last elected premier was a woman. **Unemployment is lower among women in Alberta** than for women in any other province, and Alberta couples have one of the **highest birth rates** in the country. So it would seem that in Alberta, women have a better shot than almost anywhere at a career and a family.

But Phillips doesn't see it that way. Just a couple of years ago, Phillips spoke at an Ottawa Women's Forum. The way Phillips described it, Alberta is a nightmare for women. The last thing Canadians would want is for their provinces to be more like ours, **she told the conference**. Like so many NDPers, Phillips made it clear that she isn't proud of what Albertans have built: she's ashamed of it.

At the time, Phillips was already active in the NDP. She had helped Jack Layton campaign federally in Alberta and she was communications director for the Alberta NDP until 2006. And she had worked in the war room of B.C. NDP leader Adrian Dix during the 2013 election when he ran on a platform of blocking any and all pipelines from Alberta; Dix lost, although Phillips **later said** she stands by the position since pipelines don't create legitimate jobs. Pipeliners, welders, and upstream jobs aren't legitimate according to Phillips.

In fact, Phillips thinks the entire oil sands industry is a problem: it's not the kind of place that helps women. "You rip it out, ship it out in its rawest form, extracting as little value as you can ... as quickly as possible because time is running out politically and ecologically," **she told the Women's Forum**. "We have an economic crisis in the making when we put all our eggs in this basket. For every job gained in the petroleum sector we have 30 jobs lost in the manufacturing sector."

We know that's not true. Alberta's best industry creates thousands **of jobs in manufacturing.** She sounded as if she was making a jobs argument based on recent economic data. But the reality is that Phillips had been a thorn in a side of the oil sands for some time already. She's a supporter of the Kyoto Accord, and sees the oil sands as a stain on Canada's climate change record (she **laments** Alberta's "rapidly antiquating approach to the environment and climate change" and is **dismissive about the importance of Alberta's energy** industry, calling us "a province that pays the bills by pumping CO2 into the atmosphere").

At a 2013 conference for left-wing media, she appeared on a panel that argued that the oil sands are "the source of the country's fastest-growing carbon emissions, and are having a significant impact on provincial and federal democracy, human and treaty rights, and the social fabric."

In 2008, she even travelled to Fort McMurray with Al Jazeera, the terror-promoting Qatari state broadcaster, to film an unflattering documentary on the oil sands. (As she later **recounted** in the magazine Alberta Views, she was stonewalled and it didn't work out: the provincial energy minister's assistant told her "You should try something completely different from the rest of the international media ... and do a balanced story for a change.")

Of course, even on the strictly economic facts about the oil industry's impact on women, Phillips is just dead wrong. Alberta's resource industry actually had the **fastest employment growth rate for women** of any sector in Alberta between 2004 and 2014 — a jobs growth rate of 91.5 percent. Over the same period, women were getting higher-skilled jobs, with the number of women in positions with university degrees increasing by 92.3 percent, and positions held by women with graduate degrees rising 118.5 percent.

And while it's true that Canada has seen a decline in manufacturing jobs in the last decade, primarily in Ontario and Quebec — it's actually been **far less pronounced** than in other OECD countries (including those that don't have major oil and gas industries). The reason for that, of course, is because of the rise of far-cheaper manufacturing in China. If anything, the growth of Alberta's oil sands has helped offset the decline of Canadian manufacturing, with so much of the sophisticated equipment required being provided by Canadian manufacturers. Don't take my word for it: Even the Canadian Manufacturers and Exporters group is grateful to have the oil sands: "Canadian manufacturers have a significant opportunity to not only continue selling into the oil and gas supply chains, but expanding their business as investment grows," the association wrote in **a recent report**. "Rather than having a negative impact on Canadian industry, the oil sands are providing a customer base for manufacturers."

Even if that weren't true, Canada surely has enough politicians from Ontario and Quebec advocating to shut down the oil sands in favour of redirecting jobs to Central Canada's manufacturers. We certainly don't need an Alberta cabinet minister doing it, too.

But Phillips is clearly unhappy with the success of Alberta's oil sands producers. She wants to put on the brakes: "The benefits of slowing development far outweigh the risks," she wrote in a **2012 article** called "Reality check: The NDP and the oil sands." "A slower pace of development also takes the heat off our currency, ensuring we slow the decline of the manufacturing sector, both in Alberta and the rest of Canada."

One surefire way to slow down Alberta's oil sands is by making them more expensive, which is why Phillips believes in hiking royalties. "More appropriate royalties has the effect of slowing the stampede to our currency, mitigating job losses in other parts of the country," she wrote. "Better royalties allow us to save and invest in a green economy, which is the best way to show leadership and ensure all of Canada can be put on a more sustainable path to long-term prosperity." So, Alberta should slow down so that the rest of the country can catch up? Clearly Winston Churchill had the NDP's number when he pointed out that socialism's "inherent virtue is the equal sharing of misery." Phillips would have Alberta's energy workers and their families become the sacrificial lambs to the gods of the manufacturing unions down east.

But Phillips doesn't just want to slow down the oil sands. She's succeeded in a campaign to stop a **natural gas production project** in Lethbridge. And in 2013, at the biennial convention for the Alberta Federation of Labour, where Phillips worked before winning a seat in government, **she said**: "We do not collect an appropriate royalty for either our oil sands bitumen or our conventional oil and gas reserves." In 2012, she told the **Edmonton Journal** that the provincial government not only needs higher royalties, but also needs "increased taxes on wealthy corporations and individuals."

In other words, more taxes on all oil. More taxes on all gas. And on all companies. In effect, more taxes on all jobs in Alberta. That will slow things down all right.

That might be just fine for someone who likes the idea of "keeping global capitalism away." All those lost jobs might even be considered a human moral victory for someone like Phillips, who thinks of the fight against oil and gas growth as something akin to the fight against apartheid. Or the Iraq War.

Or so she implies when she compared First Nations blockades of industrial projects to the struggles of Nelson Mandela: "Nelson Mandela didn't do 27 years in prison for sitting in the wrong seat on the bus," **Phillips said** after Mandela's death. "He was there, in part, for his role in bombing a power station in order to make the machinery of a racist regime grind to a halt ... So can we just remember that next time we see indigenous people blockading a highway?"

look at that again: Alberta's new environment minister is comparing Canada to apartheid South Africa, a country where blacks were brutalized, murdered, imprisoned and stripped of basic human rights. That's something she is willing to hold up as comparable to Canada's relationship with First Nations people.

And in the context of the oil and gas sector in Alberta, First Nations people, while less than five percent of the **Canadian population**, make up more than 10 percent of those working in the oil sands. That doesn't seem that much like apartheid.

Then there's all that First Nations wealth creation happening. From 1998 to 2010, aboriginal-owned companies secured over $5 billion worth of contracts from companies **in the oil sands region**. In fact, the Fort McKay Group of six companies, completely owned by the Fort McKay First Nations, works extensively with oil sands companies, resulting in more than $100 million in annual revenue. This is Shannon Phillips' apartheid.

And at a TED talk in Lethbridge, Phillips said **she expects** "civil disobedience" from First Nations against Alberta's Northern Gateway pipeline project — and suggested that it would be justified. Just as the anti-war movement was ultimately proven right, she insisted, when it protested the war against Saddam Hussein by the United States (Phillips, by the way, has said she thinks the U.S. is "**extraordinarily odious.**")

You see, in the great struggles of history — apartheid, Middle East tyranny — Shannon Phillips evidently views Alberta's oil and gas production and pipelines as the next frontier to fight off the malign forces of global capitalism. She'll fight against them in the name of women. She'll fight in the name of the climate. She'll fight in the name of central Canadian manufacturers. She'll fight in the name of First Nations. And she'll even fight in the name of maintaining "the social fabric."

And for those Albertans who want to keep investment coming in to support good-paying jobs? That, unfortunately, is one cause that Shannon Phillips just doesn't have the fight in her for.

CHAPTER 6

COLIN PIQUETTE

C olin Piquette is a major figure in the NDP's entrepreneur caucus. He comprises half of it, actually — being one of the paltry two elected MLAs who spent time working in business, rather than off government funding.

Before you get your hopes up, Piquette wasn't out raising investment or risking his capital on oil and gas or anything like that. He was an insurance adviser. That makes a certain amount of sense, since Piquette's view of how business operates is that he sees only negative outcomes.

In fact, it would appear that to Piquette, one of the benefits of working in the business community is that it lets him wear his suit and tie as a costume in anti-oil protests, playing the part of a sinister, environment-destroying, government-controlling capitalist — like a real-life President Business from The Lego Movie

But really, Piquette only dabbled in the insurance business for a few years. It pays the bills. His anti-oil activism is his real career passion. In 2007, at a "Justice for the Lubicon Cree" rally, Piquette put on his suit and a feathered pirate-style hat (just to be absolutely sure that there's no way anyone misses the point about the "raping and pillaging" vibe he's going for) and took part in a play about "the Republic of Greedolia." I guess we are Greedolia. One unfortunate scene in the show had Piquette **standing next** to a defaced Canadian flag: Turned upside-down, it had the words "No Justice on Stolen Land."

At another point during the protest, Piquette **took the podium** and the microphone to promise the crowd that the exploitation of native land in Alberta would become a global issue that would "be the incredible shame and detriment of this province."

He said that he'd rather "be proud of where I'm from." But in the end, he said, "How can you (be proud of Alberta)? How can you when you know that ... the province is destroying people as if they don't even exist." He said we had stolen from the Lubicon — a First Nation in northern Alberta that's clashed with government over land claims since before Piquette was born — and owed them recompense. Around him, people carried signs that read "Genocide in Our Backyards" and "No Blood for Oil" and another inverted, defaced Maple Leaf flag that read "Canada: Stop Denying Your Holocaust." Genocide, holocausts and blood for oil aren't things we do here. Alberta's competitors on the global energy market do those things.

Colin Piquette is a fifth-generation Albertan. His dad, Leo, was actually an NDP MLA in the 1980s, too — although never part of any government. Still, Piquette can't see how anyone can "be proud" of Alberta, the place that gave his family these opportunities. He can't "be proud of where I'm from."

Piquette's not a proud Albertan. And judging by his eagerness to pose alongside defaced Canadian flags, he's not big on the rest of the country, either. About a decade ago he posted a rambling, incoherent **blog** on the website of the the far-left radical publication CounterPunch about Canada "holding the bag" for the United States while they "fill it with the corpses of anyone who dares to oppose (its) God given right to tell everyone else in the world how to manage their economy and live their lives." That "we are so desperate to go back to our 'cozy' image of being the good guys again we will believe any lie that makes it seem like we are." Does Piquette still feel so angry about the Americans managing the economies of others now that Obama has vetoed Keystone XL?

Besides smearing Canada and the U.S. as generally bad guys, Piquette's point (which took some effort to locate) had to do with his belief that the U.S. had overthrown the Haitian government of Jean-Bertrand Aristide with Canada's help. He railed against both countries. He railed against business. He may have tried insurance for a few years, but what he really is a left-wing activist, opposed to oil development, who believes that Albertans are illegally occupying native land. He's even appeared at rallies alongside Tom Keefer, an anarchist who was one of the central figures in Ontario's Caledonia dispute, which saw First Nations invade and terrorize a privately owned housing development before violently attacking and evicting the white people there.

Of course, not all radical aboriginal activists turn to violence, and Piquette, who was a consultant for the City of Edmonton's "Office of Diversity of Inclusion" for five years before he gave insurance a shot, doesn't seem like the violent sort, preferring to mount plays attacking Alberta enterprise, rather than doing it literally. Still, if it's Piquette's worldview that it's time for the capitalist exploiters to pay up for what they've taken from indigenous people, then he doesn't need to resort to violence: he's got a seat in government to affect policies that might make him feel personally so terribly ashamed of being Albertan.

CHAPTER 7

LORI SIGURDSON

I t's a tough job being the Alberta minister of jobs and labour nowadays. By the time Lori Sigurdson stepped into that role, the province had already seen thousands of layoffs resulting from the collapse in oil prices. Things were about to get much worse — especially after the NDP government began pouring salt into the province's economic wounds.

A few weeks after the election, Canadian Natural Resources Ltd., one of the province's biggest private employers, announced that all the meddling in the oilpatch being proposed by the Notley government **was making it impossible to finalize its spending plans**. It had to put off meeting with investors "Due to the current uncertainty surrounding the government of Alberta's review of royalty, taxation, environmental and greenhouse gas policies."

The government had already announced **a hike in the corporate income tax**, leaving companies to cut deeper to try and eke out economic returns. It had already vowed to raise royalties on oil and gas, squeezing the battered sector even more. And in June, the NDP layered on more pain for the energy sector, **announcing a phased-in 50 percent hike in taxes on emissions for large emitters**. The government said it was pursuing a "bold and ambitious" climate change strategy. It didn't mention anything about a preserving-people's-jobs strategy.

And so, in June, TransCanada announced another 200 job cuts. A few weeks later, Cenovus, which had already cut 800 jobs earlier in the year, said it would be cutting another 300 to 400 positions. In August, ConocoPhillips Canada — which had previously cut 200 jobs — said it would have to swing the axe on another 400 employees, and 100 contractors, amounting to a 21 percent cut in its total workforce. **Shortly after that**, Penn West Petroleum announced it would have to cut loose 400 full-time employees and contractors. In Fort McMurray, the unemployment rate had risen above eight percent; it was below five percent in spring 2014. The Canadian Association of Petroleum Producers said that, by the end of summer 2015, **job losses in Alberta's oilpatch had totalled 35,000**. And there were many more guaranteed still to come.

So, in the worst recession to hit Alberta in a decade, you would think in a brutal summer of losses like that, the jobs minister would be hard at work. Perhaps pulling together a war room to find ways to stanch the jobs haemorrhage? Daily crisis meetings of her departmental staff? Certainly it calls for pulling together a roundtable of Alberta's big employers to see how the government can help them find ways to minimize further cuts.

Well, Lori Sigurdson certainly was hard at work

during Alberta's cruel summer. Just not at work in Alberta.

Sigurdson was out in B.C., working on … a political campaign. The federal NDP's political campaign. She was in the Okanagan, stumping for Thomas Mulcair. She was in a war room, alright — not to save Alberta jobs, but to get the federal NDP into power. "Creating the orange wave" in North Okanagan-Shuswap, as Sigurdson bragged on Twitter on Aug. 24. Not being in Alberta, Sigurdson missed the headline on the Calgary Herald's front page the very next day: "Oil Skid Pummels Economy."

Of course, that shouldn't come as too much of a surprise: Sigurdson didn't get into politics to help the Alberta economy. She's not a big fan of capitalism to begin with. In 2013, she actually **spoke at a forum** organized by Occupy Edmonton. Speaking in front of a banner reading "if you are not outraged, you are not paying attention," Sigurdson praised the anti-capitalist Occupy movement, which she said had "magnificently broadened the public discourses (on the) growing inequality and injustice we're experiencing." She lamented the current system that "supports the privileged few." And she actually called it a problem that Albertans have created "one of the hardest-working provinces," saying people in the province needed to spend less time working so hard. Now that she's jobs minister, she's certainly doing her part to allow Albertans the ability to work less. Or not at all.

But then, Sigurdson has also called it a problem that Albertans aren't taxed enough. "It's not really an expenditure problem in Alberta, it's a revenue problem in Alberta," she said at her **campaign launch speech in March 2015** (despite the fact that the **province's per capita program spending** was nearly 40 percent higher than B.C.'s in 2013–14 and second only to Newfoundland for being the highest in the country, according to data from RBC Economics). "We know that we're taxed $11 billion less than any other jurisdiction in Canada." Taxes, she said, "are neither good nor bad." Yet she called low taxes "an ideological choice" by the PC government — and one that had to be changed.

And by devoting her energies to Thomas Mulcair, instead of Albertans, Sigurdson was helping to make it a reality that there would be a federal party in government that has expressed support for a moratorium on new oil sands projects. One of Mulcair's key Toronto candidates **declared during the election that**, to meet the NDP's climate goals, "a lot of the oil sands oil may have to stay in the ground."

But that's nothing compared to the jobs-killing, anti-oil position of the NDP member that Sigurdson was helping to campaign in North Okanagan-Shuswap. Jacqui Gingras is an even bigger environmental extremist than the NDP candidates in downtown Toronto. In 2014, **she helped orga-**

nize an anti-pipeline protest, working with the American anti-oil sands group LeadNow — the radical group that shamed Tim Hortons into cancelling an advertising deal with Enbridge. When Vernon's Morning Star newspaper reported in 2014 that Gingras would seek the NDP candidacy for the local riding, it reported that, "Gingras has a professional background in nutrition and has campaigned for climate justice with LeadNow, for a fair economy with the Occupy movement, and for indigenous treaty rights with Idle No More."

So the Alberta NDP's minister of jobs backs anti-pipeline, anti-oil and anti-capitalist causes. She is averse to low taxes and has a problem with Albertans working too much. Believing all that, maybe it shouldn't surprise us that she didn't spend the summer of layoffs at work in Alberta throwing her efforts into stemming the crisis. With the entire province's economy breaking down, and more and more Albertans finding equality on the unemployment line, to Sigurdson, everything must look like it's going just according to plan.

CHAPTER 8

DAVE MOWAT

A lbertans aren't fools. We know that a left-wing government only launches a "review" of oil and gas royalties with one purpose in mind: to raise taxes on the oil and gas industry. Even Tory premier Ed Stelmach was set on a plan to take a bigger slice for government when he launched his royalty review in 2007 — although he was at least reasonable enough to realize eventually that he'd gone too far, and reversed his review panel's royalty increases two years later. Of course, that was only after driving energy business and jobs into the arms of neighbouring states and provinces.

The NDP has been clear about the fact that it plans to take more money away from Alberta operators. And maybe you even think they're right to do it. Lots of Tory voters supported Stelmach's review, too. The ones that didn't went on to form the Wildrose Party.

But the NDP wants you to think their royalty review will somehow be "fair." And they expect you to believe it. During the election campaign, Rachel Notley made it sound so benign when she was warned that another royalty review, especially during an oil crash, would once again damage the industry. "I don't exactly know how a review would be devastating one way or another," **she said**. "I don't know how talking to Albertans, with Albertans, in an independent, transparent, accountable forum about a resource that belongs to Albertans is going to kill the industry." Just talking, she says.

Her energy minister, Margaret McCuaig-Boyd, was a bit more honest — it's about getting more money. "Are we getting our fair share? Could it be different?" she said. And then there's the brutally honest NDPers, like environment minister Shannon Phillips, who **has said**, "We do not collect an appropriate royalty for either our oil sands bitumen or our conventional oil and gas reserves," and **talked about** using higher royalties to slow oil sands development and spending the money on building a "green" economy. And don't forget Rod "60 percent royalties" Loyola. We know where he stands.

The NDP needed to appear like it was launching a fair royalty review — while actually making sure that it would end up with higher royalties to slow down the fossil-fuel economy and fund subsidies for the global-warming cause.

So it turned to Dave Mowat.

The NDP's appointment of Dave Mowat, the president and CEO of the provincially owned ATB Financial, to head the royalty review panel actually relieved some worried Albertans. That's what his appointment was supposed to do; to placate.

He has "has proven himself 100 times over to

the Alberta business community and the community-at-large, transforming the once-stodgy financial institution into a competitive banking house that walks the walk and talks the talk when it comes to customer service, employee satisfaction and community outreach," wrote Graham Hicks in The Edmonton Sun's "Hicks on Biz." In another column, Hicks called Mowat the "the last thing from (a) left-wing ideologue ... and the closest thing to good ol' common sense."

The Edmonton Journal called Mowat the "business-friendly face of the province's royalty review advisory panel."

So the NDP got what it wanted: a chief royalty reviewer that hasn't raised anyone's suspicions about an anti-oil agenda.

But he should.

Dave Mowat is as much a fanatic about climate change as the most left-wing NDPer.

He transferred to ATB Financial from Vancouver, where he ran the Vancity credit union. While there, he launched his own foundation — **the Dave Mowat Climate Change Endowment Fund** — dedicated to "help ameliorate the effects of climate change."

Two of the biggest enemies of Alberta's economy in B.C. are Carol Newell and Joel Solomon, the wealthy and connected power donors that have helped the Tides Foundation launder millions of foreign dollars into Canada and into the pockets of the most extremist anti-oil groups in the country. At Vancity, Mowat **got involved** with both of them through their company **Renewal Partners**. In a profile of Newell, who is said to be an heiress of the U.S. Rubbermaid fortune, the Vancouver Sun quoted Mowat praising the work of Renewal:

"What also makes Renewal unique in B.C., (Dave) Mowat says, is that when it is considering investing in a new business, the most important criterion on which it bases its decision is not whether the business will make money ... but how it will contribute to the greater good," wrote reporter Nicholas Read in 2005.

Vancity ended up making a deal with Renewal Partners in a "socially responsible portfolio management service" called Real Assets — a partnership **that reserved a portion of profits** specifically for the anti-oil sands Tides Foundation. In other words, Dave Mowat's idea of using profits to "contribute to the greater good" meant funnelling those profits to Tides priorities. Campaigns like the "**Week to End Enbridge**" and the "**Tanker Free Coast campaign**."

Mowat himself not only **donates personally** to Tides, he was nominated by Tides to be a member of an "Expert Panel on Social Finance" that the eco-radical group had lobbied the Canadian government to establish.

In Vancouver, Solomon and Newell are known as leaders of what's called the "**Hollyhock Mafia**," named after the Cortes Island "educational" retreat, the Hollyhock Centre, whose mission is "to inspire, nourish and support people who are making the world better." Or, as the National Post once described it, "a New Age retreat known for its holistic healing circles, Shaman drum-making workshops and Tantric 'sacred sexuality' seminars." It acts as a headquarters for the radical B.C. left, drawing to its "Social Change Institute" leading members of ForestEthics, the Dogwood Initiative, and Environmental Defence — all groups zealously devoted to demonizing and shutting down Alberta's oil sands. In attendance, also, at the Social Change Institute? **Dave Mowat**.

You see, Dave Mowat isn't just a bank CEO. He's a major player in the Canadian environmentalist movement. Who said money guys can't live on the far left?

He is Al Gore in Alberta.

That sounds like an exaggeration. But Mowat was actually hand picked by Al Gore's global warming group to train as a "climate-change warrior," as **an article in BCBusiness** magazine explained in 2007. "The goal of Gore's boot camps is to train societal leaders from across North America before dispatching them to spread the gospel of global warming with their own 'core Gore' versions of the presentation featured in An Inconvenient Truth," the alarmist global warming/anti-oil film.

Out of an estimated 1,000 Canadian applicants at the time, Mowat was just one of 18 to have earned a spot. Gore coached Mowat and the others through the entire Inconvenient Truth presentation. They all made a commitment to take the presentation home with them and give a minimum number of talks to convert more believers to the Gore camp (Mowat would make the Gore speech to Vancity credit-union employees, the Vancouver Board of Trade, the World Council of Credit Unions, a Health Sciences Association of B.C. conference, a group of parliamentarians in Ottawa, and the school board of Terrace, B.C.). This sounds a lot like a home-based business scheme blown up on a grander scale.

Mowat sat down with BCBusiness to detail his "personal evolution to environmental warrior ... from being a skeptic to a reluctant but curious observer to a full-blown convert."

That interview took place just as Mowat was preparing to move from Vancouver to take the helm of ATB Financial in Edmonton. At one point, the reporter pauses to wonder if Mowat "will continue his climate-change crusade in Alberta, a jurisdiction far less amenable to tough talk on the environment and also home to the greenhouse-gas-belching oil-sands sector."

Mowat tells him he isn't worried. "I don't think it matters whether you're in B.C., Ontario or Alberta; people are interested in this issue. I've got a huge job and learning curve ahead of me, so I won't prejudge what kind of role I'll play at this point."

Who would have imagined back then that his

role would be having the power to turn the screws as tightly as he wants on Alberta's oil and gas industry?

CHAPTER 9

THE BUDGET

T he job losses just kept coming into the fall. When normally energy companies are ramping up for the busy winter drilling season with new hires and new equipment, they were, instead, quietly holding tense meetings and giving out pink slips.

During all this time, the NDP delayed their first budget when Alberta companies needed certainty the most. A fierce federal election campaign was underway and the NDP mother party was looking to replicate the fluke success of Notley's party. A bad Alberta budget would hurt Thomas Mulcair's chances nationally and so the NDP tried to gather federal votes at the expense of Alberta jobs. Albertans would have to keep waiting until Mulcair's fate was known.

He lost. But Albertans did, too.

Albertans wanted to be wrong about what they were coming to know about the NDP and it's anti-oil, anti-business and frankly, anti-Albertan agenda. But Albertans are realists. The run up to the budget felt like a long wait to remove a bandage. It was going to hurt, Albertans knew that much. But how much blood would there be?

Then the budget came out.

Notley's first budget saw the largest deficit in Alberta's history at $26.8 billion over the next three years, bringing Alberta to a record $47.4 billion in debt by 2019. The debt servicing costs alone (at a triple A credit rating) amount to $1.3 billion by 2017. In fact, Alberta is now **outspending our more populous neighbour, B.C.,** by about 6.5 billion dollars per year. In more practical terms, Alberta spends $1,500 more per person than B.C. You couldn't argue B.C is some underfunded, Third World dump. So what do we have to show for all that spending?

What we have to show is a well-fed public sector. In fact, it's bloated. The budget was rife with big spending and rewards for the public-sector unions that worked so hard to get the NDP elected. While the private sector spent the summer hemorrhaging jobs, the NDP was scheming to throw more money at their public-sector union pals in health care and education. It almost seemed like the Alberta Union of Public Employees had written the budget themselves.

Think that sounds crazy and a touch conspiratorial? Maybe. But Notley and Finance Minister Ceci called their inaugural budget "The Alberta Way." If that sounds familiar, it's because "The Alberta Way" is a registered trademark of the AUPE. The slogan was used on a now defunct AUPE website and in a series of anti-conservative rallies.

Then there's Mark Wells. He's the new head of the non-partisan communications arm of the Alberta government known as the Parliamentary Affairs Bureau. Mark Wells, before he had his new job — one that pays him a comfortable $217,586 this year — was the senior communications advisor to the Alberta Union of Provincial Employees. That was during the time the union was using the Alberta Way Slogan. Oh, and Mark Wells used to be the director of communications for the **provincial NDP**.

In four years, will we be able to tell where the public-sector unions end and the government begins? The public sector, once a hungry little piglet, is now one of the big pigs; living in the farmer's house, wearing his clothes.

In the budget, there were also raises to the fuel tax and raises to sin taxes on **cigarettes and liquor**. Never have Albertans needed a drink more. Remember, Alberta declared the provincial debt paid in full on July 13, 2004. That work, that careful sacrifice? It's all gone.

The consequences of the NDP's "attack budget" started rolling in almost immediately.

Within minutes of the budget coming down, Shell had pulled the plug on its multi-billion dollar Carmon Creek project, one already $2 billion into construction. They walked away from 80,000 barrels per day and 1,450 Alberta jobs. Shell cited uncertainty around pipeline capacity as one of the main reasons for halting **the project.** With all of the anti-pipeline activists in the NDP, including the premier herself, Shell's concerns seem well placed.

The day after the budget, MEG Energy announced a loss of nearly half a billion dollars and layoffs of 30 percent **of their staff**. And MEG cut their capital expenditures from over a billion dollars to just $200 million.

But industry wasn't done. The dominos began to fall everywhere in the immediate days that followed the budget.

Cenovus announced it would be laying off 700 more people in addition to the 800 it had already laid off. And Devon Energy announced it would be laying off 200 people. Then Husky Energy announced that they'd laid off 1,400 staff and would be selling off its **Alberta assets.**

TransAlta, the power giant, announced they were cancelling their massive **Sundance 7** natural gas electricity generating plant on Oct. 30. They parked their $1.6 billion project on the shelf until the next decade, citing an uncertain royalty regime and greenhouse gas policy. Sundance 7 had cleared its final environmental hurdle on Oct. 20. But then the budget happened. At least TransAlta is optimistic. The next decade will be just after the end of Notley's rule in Alberta.

Albertans in the days and weeks that followed the attack budget saw the birth of a capital strike. In a regular strike, workers withhold labour. In a capital strike, companies withhold investment. And were they ever. Companies that normally ramp up spending for the winter drill season were cutting back on spending and staff as much as they could. And the ones that could just up and leave Alberta did. I mean, if you didn't have to do business here, would you?

Even Moody's, the credit rating agency, warned that all this wild spending would damage Alberta's AAA **credit rating.** And a credit downgrade makes servicing Alberta's ballooning debt that much more expensive.

If you wanted to draw a road map to the end of energy sector in Alberta, this pro-union, pro-environmentalist, anti-business budget was it. And it looks like it's working so far.

CHAPTER 10

BILL 6

When Albertans elected a new NDP government on the prairie, they had reason to assume they were at least getting the prairie version of the NDP. That is, the party of Roy Romanow and Lorne Calvert in Saskatchewan. An NDP that could be a bit kooky about a lot of things, sure, but at least a populist, farmer-friendly kind of NDP. After all, the NDP started in the farm belt — when its predecessor, the Co-operative Commonwealth Federation, was founded in Calgary as a party out to help farmers hurt by the Great Depression.

But what Albertans got was something else. What they elected was a Brian Topp NDP — an NDP run out of the far left, anti-oil sands, public-sector-unionized urban east. Case in point: Saskatchewan's NDP actually had farmers in their caucus. Heck, even Ontario's NDP has rural farmers in its caucus. But Alberta's NDP? Nope. Not a single one.

So what do you get when you have a bunch of radical left-wing government-union activists like Brian Topp running a government in a western prairie province? You get a law that lets big city union bosses onto the farms. You get Bill 6.

Bill 6 is officially called the Enhanced Protection for Farm and Ranch Workers Act. That makes it sound like a law designed to improve farm safety. Hey, that sounds good. We all want everyone to be safe on the farm. What could be wrong with a law designed to do that?

Except that's not really what Bill 6 is meant to do. What it's really meant to do is destroy the family farm culture in Alberta and replace it with a collectivized union culture.

And it does it in just 14 words.

Really — that's how brief the first part of Bill 6 is. The most dangerous part. All it says is this:

1 (1) "The Employment Standards Code is amended by this section."

2 (2): "Section 2(3) and (4) are repealed."

That's it.

Of course, it's easier and takes less time — also, fewer words — to destroy something than it does to build something. The World Trade Center took nearly four years to build, but just a day to demolish. Alberta's rural way of life is something our province has been building on for more than a century. And with just 14 words, Bill 6 is blowing it up.

Here's what Bill 6 does by repealing sections 2(3) and (4) of the Employment Standards Code: it takes away from family farms the right to run themselves like actual farms. It takes away the exemptions that were designed specifically to make room for the special circumstances of running a farm. Farms aren't factories, of course. They run according to weather and the seasons, and the days can be long during seeding and harvest time, and much shorter in the winter. That's why farms have long been exempted from commercial-workplace rules that might make sense for office or retail workers, but make no sense on a farm. Rules that limit how long someone can work, regulate overtime and overtime pay, require vacations and statutory holidays. And laws that prohibit anyone working who's under 18 years old. You know, like farm kids.

In short, Bill 6 — with its rules about working hours and holiday pay — has nothing to do with "farm safety," as the NDP pretends. It's a law to ban the family farm.

If you know any farmers — and if you've lived in Alberta for any length of time you probably do — you might know that whether they run a big farm or a small farm, it's a family affair. There isn't a family farm in this province where everyone, young and old, doesn't pitch in when things get hectic. Like when an animal is sick, or giving birth, or has run away, or there's fieldwork that needs to be done while the weather's still co-operating. The farmer isn't just a worker who commutes to the ranch from a condo down the highway. These families live on the farm for a reason: it's where they all work, day and night.

It's not a business where people go home after work. Farming is a 24-hour a day, 365-day a year job. Cows still have to be fed on Labour Day. The harvest still needs to come in, even if it's after quitting time.

So Bill 6 is what happens when agriculture policy falls into the hands of people who have only worked in unionized government workplaces, where they wander in at 10, leave at four, and have mandated coffee and lunch breaks, paid vacations, and professional sensitivity training sessions. And this NDP government is a government of union bosses. Not farmers. Rachel Notley's husband is a union boss with the Canadian Union of Public Employees — government workers. Her chief of staff is a boss with the Toronto-based union for TV and movie actors. These people don't have a clue about farm life. No one in the caucus does, because none of them farm. In a province where one-third of the population is rural, that's just statistically bizarre. How did we manage to elect 54 NDP MLAs and yet not a single actual farmer? That's as weird as if Newfoundlanders had elected an entire government without a single MLA who had ever set foot on a boat.

There's a second part of Bill 6, though. It amends the Labour Relations Code to require the family farm to respect minimum wage laws. As if a cattle ranch is the same as a Burger King. There's no clock to punch you in and out on a farm. You work before breakfast, and after dinner. Farmers never stop working. And the kids work, too. So now, mom and dad have to pay minimum wage to their kids? Assuming their kids are legally of age to work on the farm, that is. This isn't a farm policy; it's a Joseph Heller novel.

But of course the NDP had to include minimum wage. Minimum wage is the secret weapon for unions, because it keeps low-cost labour from taking jobs and drives up province-wide wages, which helps unions agitate for more money when they're bargaining for a new contract.

But on the farm, that low-wage labour isn't going to be filled by lunchbox-toting Teamsters. It's the kids. It's their friends. It's the neighbours who come over to help, because tomorrow, they're going to need some help, too. Families that have lived next to each other for generations who have been pitching in on each others' farms for just as long. But in Rachel Notley's Alberta, something as normal, traditional, and human as a bunch of wives cooking a big dinner while the husbands harvest the fields, well, that's now going to be subject to minimum wage, and overtime, and vacation pay. Which is so impossible to make work in practice, so illogical, so unfeasible, that it can't even be done. So, in other words, it must stop. It has to be banned. Kids working on farms: banned by child labour laws. Families helping each other out: banned by minimum wage laws.

The family farm: banned by Alberta's NDP.

And they claim this is a bill about "farm safety."

You see, it's not only that the NDP doesn't understand farms — they also don't like what our rural life represents. Farmers represent a pretty un-pretentious form of capitalism. There's a freedom to being a farmer, as most owners will attest. And there's that independent rural streak that sees a lot more value in the family unit and community than in big government. It's a big part of what helped create Alberta's self-reliant culture. That's what the NDP can't stand.

Just take a look at the third part of Bill 6, which repeals farm exemptions from the Occupational Health and Safety Act. Farmers have always been exempt from workers compensation schemes. All farmers. That doesn't mean farms don't already have private insurance. They do. But letting the private market solve things isn't something the NDP can stand. This, after all, is their way of collectivizing Alberta's farms — bringing these untamed institutions under the control of government. Socialists have never trusted employers or even parents to make decisions. Hey, what do farmers know about looking after the safety and health of their kids compared to the benevolent wisdom of the nanny state?

Except, Alberta's nanny state is far more dangerous than any farm. Because the province literally does sometimes act as a caretaker for kids — children who come into their care through the child welfare program. And in the past year, 33 children being "taken care of" by the province's system died. Another 11 were seriously injured. That's an average casualty rate of one kid a week — an even faster clip than the rate at which aboriginal women in this country are being murdered, if you're looking to compare social ills or for things that could stand a thorough inquiry. That's the safe, secure, caring embrace of the unionized nanny state: after it assumes responsibility for kids that need help, an alarming number of them end up in the hospital or the morgue.

These are the people that claim they can run a family farm better than Albertan families can.

Obviously no one outside the NDP actually believes that. Alberta farms have been going strong for over a century. No one thinks that the government imposing minimum wage and vacation pay and workers compensation and unionization is actually going to improve our farms, let alone that these changes have anything to do with "farm safety."

This has to do with attacking the last bastion of true freedom in Alberta — the countryside. A countryside made up of farms and ranches who, notably, did not vote NDP in the last election. This is a solution looking for a problem — and the problem that Rachel Notley sees is that farmers are independent, unshackled by big government restrictions, union free ... and actually doing just fine that way.

Just like there was no real problem with the oilpatch, before Notley decided to come along and fix it. The problem, in Notley's mind, is the oilpatch. The problem is the farm. To Rachel Notley, the problem is everything that made Alberta what it is

— a province that values entrepreneurialism over subsidization, and unionization and freedom over regulation. That's what she really wants to stop.

CHAPTER 11

CARBON TAX

I n the 2008 federal election, Albertans sensibly voted to give the Liberals exactly zero seats in their province. Just 11 percent of Albertans voted for the party led by Stéphane Dion, which was only slightly more than voted Green, but actually less than the number who voted for the New Democrats. There were good reasons for that. For one thing, the Liberal brand has been in terrible odour in Alberta since Pierre Trudeau took the province's oilpatch hostage in the early 1980s with his National Energy Program, destroying businesses, jobs and people's lives and families in the process. For another thing, Dion was planning something that looked awfully similar: a carbon tax. Or — eventually called what it was — a tax on everything.

Almost precisely seven years after Dion's defeat, Albertans were duped into saddling themselves with the very same terrible policies that the federal Liberals had designed to whack their province with: a tax on everything — and one that would run the oilpatch into the ground faster than even the National Energy Program.

Rachel Notley did not mention anything about a carbon tax in her election. She wasn't elected to slap a tax to deliver a body blow to our vital energy sector even as it's already reeling from so many other brutal conditions. But she went ahead and used her obsessive climate scaremongering to do it anyway: a tax paid by everyone of $30 per tonne of CO_2, quickly rising to $50 a tonne — or, put more simply, $3 to $5 billion a year in extra taxes sucked out of the pockets of workers and businesses.

This is a carbon tax on everything. On oil, on natural gas, on gasoline at the pump, on home heating fuel, on anything that moves, or anything that has to stay warm in the winter. Notley says it's going to cost every Alberta home $500 a year, quickly rising to $900 bucks a year. That's just about what an average family in Canada pays in GST. Now, Notley just added her own brand new sales tax, just as big as the federal one, but applied to even more products: it's the NDP GST. Except, unlike the original GST, this one is set to keep going up, and up, and up, at a rate of two percent every year.

In 2015, 100,000 Albertans lost their jobs thanks to the crisis in the oilpatch. And that was before Notley told investors and employers that, even though they're losing money at oil prices at a third of what they were just a year earlier and natural gas prices at rock bottom rates, they will now also have to pay higher taxes on every drop they produce. And ship. And process. In the name of the climate. Soon 100,000 lost jobs will look like nothing. Expect that number to double in 2016. We're talking more jobs lost than under Trudeau's original NEP.

But all those lost jobs aren't even just a side effect of Notley's climate plan: they're part of the design. Remember that the NDP's goal is to get Alberta out of the oil and gas business. Notley came right out and said her climate policy is meant to "help people reduce their energy use." Now, imagine a Saskatchewan premier asking people to cut grain out of their diet. Notley wants to lead the world by example in showing how we can get off fossil fuels — the most crucial product we make. And she'll keep loading on the taxes until Albertans can't even afford to buy them.

Plus, she's just going to outright ban by 2030 all the jobs in Alberta's coal-power industry, which gives the province half its electricity. Albertans rely on clean coal for cheap, reliable power — and as an important part of our economy. But because Notley personally prefers wind power and solar power, she thinks she's entitled to just command us to close up our coal industry and fire everyone who works in it within the next decade and half.

Notley wants to force us to "replace two-thirds of our existing coal electricity with renewable energy." Of course, that means subsidized renewable energy — because wind farms and solar power just aren't anything close to economical compared to fossil fuels. That's why Ontario now has the highest electricity prices in North America — the government there ordered coal plants shut down, too, claiming the province would be better off with renewables. That didn't happen. Once Canada's industrial heartland, Ontario is watching factories closing down every month because they simply can't pay the price of the "green" electricity that politicians wanted, but everyone else can't afford.

And in the oil sands, Notley didn't even disguise the fact that she wants to thwart the growth of the industry: She actually put a ceiling on how much bigger the oil sands can get. She told producers that they she will only let them have a bit more room to grow their CO_2 emissions — to a maximum of 100 megatonnes per year (and we're already at 70 megatonnes) — and that's it. After that, they must stop, no matter how much the world may want to pay us to produce more oil. And she cut a special deal with just four producers — Shell Canada, Cenovus, Canadian Natural Resources, and Suncor — who will get to carve up that one last piece of growth between them, to get them to support her plan.

That's already set off a civil war in the oilpatch between those producers and the ones who got cut out of the deal. Of course it has. The oil sands are a hostage to the NDP — they can't just pick up their rigs and move. And so Notley told her captives there would be no more rations for anyone — but then promised just one last little morsel to just a few producers to share. So now we have a premier who's out to turn Alberta's economy into her own sick version of the Hunger Games.

She has, after all, decided which sectors she will allow to thrive and which she wants to watch die. Coal will be banned. And for some reason the oil sands faces that emission cap, which makes it the only sector in the province singled out that way. As if a tonne of CO_2 emitted from an oil sands plant is somehow less righteous than all the CO_2 emitted from a trucking company, or from a furnace, or your car.

But to Notley there is a difference: oil is central to Alberta's way of life, and the oil sands are central to Alberta's future as an energy power. She knows that, if she doesn't stand in the way, the province's energy sector will keep growing richer and more powerful, all thanks to the amazing natural resources we've been blessed with. That's the future that anti-oil radicals — the environment minister's friends at Greenpeace, Tides, Environmental Defence, the Pembina Institute, and Graham Mitchell's comrades at LeadNow — have been trying to stop Alberta from ever seeing. And they're counting on their friends in the NDP to deliver that lethal blow to Alberta's potential. Rachel Notley knows she has just a short period of time to do it — to kill off our coal industry, to divide and conquer our oil sands industry, and to force Albertans into weaning themselves off the very products that our economy relies on.

That's why the premier of a carbon-based economy has declared a war on carbon. She might claim to do it in the name of helping the climate, yet, Alberta's contribution to global CO_2 emissions is so small that even if you accept the most over-the-top theories of man-made climate change, none of this — the oil sands caps, the carbon tax on everything, the banning of coal power — will cool the climate by even a hundredth of a degree. Not even the premier has been so audacious as to suggest it will. What this NDP "climate plan" will do is ravage Alberta's economy and jobs and businesses and our quality of life. Which is exactly how Notley wants it.

CONCLUSION: WAVE OF DESTRUCTION

All the loony Marxists you've read about in these pages, the oilpatch-hating eco-radicals, the anti-capitalist Occupy backers, the wealth haters, the people who would outlaw cars, the royalty grabbers, the high-tax crusaders, the Al Gore disciples — Rachel Notley wants to pretend they all don't exist. She really expects us to believe that her government isn't the most radical thing to hit Alberta since the Cretaceous-Tertiary extinction.

Life for the oil companies is "going to be just A-OK over here in Alberta," she lied, **just hours after her election**. Dave Mowat, the CEO of Crown-owned ATB Financial, predicted to the Edmonton Journal in June that his "guess" about the NDP was that "they'll be surprisingly business friendly. I think their goal is to create stability in the province, and that's what the business community wants."

Three weeks later, Notley appointed Mowat — a.k.a the Grand Poobah of the Alberta chapter of Al Gore's Inconvenient Truth cult — to lead the review to decide just how painfully the government should squeeze new royalties out of oil and gas employers; the employers that remain, that is.

And that same month, Notley raised taxes on businesses and the skilled workers of Fort McMurray. And she whacked oil and gas producers with a new carbon tax that will see the rates companies pay double. Then, just weeks later, she announced that in addition to her opposition to pipelines that would export crude to international markets through B.C. and the U.S., **she would also now be taking her orders** from the Liberals in Quebec and Ontario on whether Alberta would back the Energy East pipeline to New Brunswick.

Notley is in a breakneck race to hammer our energy industry as hard and fast as possible. It sure as heck isn't what anyone would call "stability." And, sorry Dave, it's pretty much the exact opposite of "what the business community wants."

That's the thing about NDP politicians: they try to get us to believe they're business friendly, but the fact is that — if you take away near-deathbed conversion of the last Saskatchewan NDP government — they never are.

Not in B.C., where the party's leader Adrian Dix thankfully ended up revealing his true "ban-everything" face to the province before getting properly clobbered in an election he seemed at one point dangerously close to winning. Not in Ontario, where voters are still terrified of a repeat of the Bob Rae years. And not in Alberta under Rachel the Revolutionary.

Whatever bluffing they do before they get into power, the reality is that NDPers are enormously proud of being socialists. Their hostility to business and wealth creation is at the very core of their ideology. Inscribed on NDP party membership cards in Manitoba is the credo "Our society must change from one based on competition to one of cooperation ... where individuals give according to their abilities and receive according to their needs." That's straight-up channelling Karl Marx. The NDP doesn't want to be in power to improve our current economic system; it wants to turn our system upside down.

It isn't for nothing that Ontario has been refused to entertain returning to an NDP government for more than 20 years. That B.C. has held its nose and clung to often-unpalatable Liberal governments for more than 14 years, dreading the NDP alternative. That Saskatchewanians are so relieved to have a sensible conservative in Brad Wall, after 16 years of NDP rule, that, for years, his popularity ratings have topped that of every other premier in the country. Here's just a quick look at the wonderful economic record of provinces under NDP rule:

> - While in the care of NDP premiers Mike Harcourt, Glen Clark, Dan Miller and Ujjal Dosanjh, B.C. saw its debt, as a percentage of GDP, rise from 10.6 to 18.2 percent — a stunning 72 percent growth in public indebtedness. Meanwhile, families saw their income growth rate lag substantially below the Canadian average, by about half.

> - The legacy of B.C.'s NDP was **summed up in a report** by Canada's foremost econ-

omist, Jack Mintz, who found that in the mid-Nineties, as British Columbia's NDP was in its first few years of power, B.C. and Alberta had roughly the same amount of just over 16 percent of the country's annual private capital investment. Then came many more years of NDP rule, and by 2001, when the NDP was finally voted out of office, B.C was down to 11 percent. (Alberta's share continued to rise — only partly due to oil and gas investment — to reach 27 percent by 2011). We used to call this the Alberta advantage.

- In Saskatchewan, under a succession of NDP leaders, the province saw its population shrink, as nearly 80,000 people — many of them the province's best and brightest workers — fled the province seeking better economic opportunities elsewhere, like Alberta. (The out-migration trend reversed only after Wall's Saskatchewan Party took office). Like Notley wants to, the Saskatchewan NDP tried imposing a punitive royalty rate on oil and gas, driving private interests out of the province. That let the NDP government step in and create a state-owned oil company, SaskOil. Salaries in Saskatchewan's oil and gas industry lagged far below those in the industry elsewhere. (The last NDP premier, Lorne Calvert, finally agreed to lower royalties — about 20 years later.)

- Under 15 years of NDP rule in Manitoba, the province went from a budget surplus of $11 million to a deficit weighing in at a whopping $451 million. No wonder: program spending in that province climbed a dizzying 87 percent. Meanwhile, tens of thousands of people continue to abandon the province for more promising pastures; 80,000 just since Greg Selinger was elected in 2009 and many more before that. That's why the province's recorded unemployment rate is actually deceptive. When you count all those workers who left Manitoba for jobs, the jobless rate isn't really 5.2 percent; it's more like 13.8 percent.

- Revealing the horrifying extent that an NDP catastrophe can take on when it strikes a province with real economic power — not unlike Alberta — Ontarians watched their province's fiscal deficit swell nearly three times as large under Bob Rae's leadership, from losing $3.3 billion a year to $8.8 billion a year. Rae engorged the province's debt as a percentage of GDP by a shocking 126 percent — a debt burden the province is still paying off a generation later. Not surprisingly, the stagnation saw unemployment rise 2.5 times faster than the national rate. Income taxes were ratcheted up for every income bracket, resulting in the province boasting the highest income tax in all of North America — by a significant amount. Meanwhile, median family income fell at a rate greater than the national average. More jobs were lost in Ontario than at any point since the Great Depression. By the time Rae left office, an appalling 1.2 million Ontarians were on welfare.

So much for the notion of the "business friendly" NDP. Of the 11 provincial NDP premiers this country has seen, only four outperformed the national average in terms of reducing unemployment. The others — nearly two-thirds — made unemployment worse than the national average. Nine of the 11 premiers ended their terms leaving their province's family incomes worse off than the national average.

And these are just the lowest-lights of provincial NDP policies past. There are many more ugly economic stories left behind when the dangerous orange wave finally recedes from a province — like soggy garbage washed up on the beach — than there are positive ones.

More importantly, this is what happened to provinces where the NDP government wasn't actually at war with the very industries that are the lifeblood of job creation. Bob Rae's government actually had policies to subsidize manufacturing (even if they ended up making the economic problems worse). In B.C., the NDP subsidized the natural resource sector. In Saskatchewan, the NDP and farmers were like peas in a pod.

These weren't NDP governments that were ashamed of their economies, like Rachel Notley's team is. They didn't storm into power on vows to directly try shutting down vital employment projects, the way Notley and Co. want to suspend oil sands approvals. Previous NDP governments supported their provinces' exports — unlike Notley's hostility to exporting Alberta oil. They would never have even dreamed of banning the very products that create demand for their province's goods, the way that Brian Topp dreams of outlawing gasoline-powered cars.

We have seen the damage that inept, wrongheaded NDP policies can do. We can only imagine the kind of carnage that awaits when an NDP government like Alberta's is determined to deliberately sabotage its most important business interests.

Rachel Notley has imposed a carbon tax and sentenced our coal industry and power plants to death. She's imposed the "tax on everything" that even Liberals learned to fear. She has already raised taxes on corporations. She's raised taxes on skilled workers in the oilpatch. She's doubling the cost of carbon-dioxide emissions for oil and gas producers. She's getting ready to unleash higher royalties. And she wants to jack up the minimum wage by nearly 50 percent, to $15 an hour, the highest in the country. She's declared war on our family farms.

And she's only been in office a few months.

This is just getting started, and already the province is seeing so many jobs and so much wealth go up in smoke as the NDP pours so much socialist fuel onto the fire of an already-severe oil crisis.

The destruction has only just begun. Left unchecked, the NDP will drive the province deeper into the red. The economy will bleed jobs and investment. This wave that has crashed over Alberta with the election of Rachel Notley's NDP isn't an orange one; it's crimson.

ABOUT THE AUTHOR

Sheila Gunn-Reid is the Alberta bureau chief for TheRebel.media. She's a stay at home mom of three and a conservative activist. Sheila grew up on the family farm and she has strong ties to the oil patch.

Sheila has been a contributor to Corus radio's Roy Green Show, where she was part of the Hockey Mom's Panel, tackling issues like government over-reach and encroachment into our families.

You can reach her at **Sheila@TheRebel.media**

ABOUT
THEREBEL.MEDIA

TheRebel.media is Canada's only independent source of news, opinion and activism. Launched by Ezra Levant and Brian Lilley after the Sun News Network shut down, The Rebel has become essential for anyone looking for "the other side of the story".

Made in the USA
Middletown, DE
03 October 2016